by Fred Smith

Rollerdrome and the Millionaire: Poems (2002)

FRED SMITH

ROLLERDROME AND THE MILLIONAIRE

POEMS

BLACK SPARROW PRESS

SANTA ROSA • 2002

ACKNOWLEDGMENTS

Grateful acknowledgment is made to the following for permission to use previously published material in "Seven Japanese Portraits": Charles E. Tuttle Co., Inc., Tokyo; Columbia University Press, New York; and Roger Peneau.

Some of these poems first appeared in *Bay Windows, Coastlines, Exquisite Corpse,* and *The New Blind Date.*

Black Sparrow Press books are printed on acid-free paper.

Cover art by Yasuhiro Esaki.

LIBRARY OF CONGRESS CATALOGING-IN-PUBLICATION DATA

Smith, Fred, 1933–
    Rollerdrome and the millionaire : poems / Fred Smith.
      p. cm.
    ISBN 1-57423-183-9 (paperback)
    ISBN 1-57423-184-7 (cloth trade)
    ISBN 1-57423-185-5 (signed cloth)
      I. Title.
    PS3619.M585 R65 2002
    811'.6—dc21   2002018479

for Yasuhiro Esaki

Contents

Seven Japanese Portraits

Rollerdrome and the Millionaire

ROLLERDROME
AND THE
MILLIONAIRE

CHILDREN, PARENTS AND OTHER OBSERVATIONS

1 They were waiting in the airport
the same as I was. For a plane
that was already one hour late,
and not expected to arrive
for forty-five more minutes. The
boy was reading a newspaper.
Blond and very good looking in
sweater and Levis. Sunglasses
hanging from the collar of his
sweater. The woman also
wearing Levis. A silk or rayon
cowboy shirt with rows of pearl
buttons that snap, on the cuffs and
on the flaps over the pockets.
A red face with prominent
cheekbones and stringy yellow hair.

They were flirting with each other,
telling jokes and making remarks,
laughing together the way
women who live without husbands
come to depend on their sons for
company. "I don't want to hear
you say that again for at least
five years." "Do you think he will be
wearing his uniform?" Just who
were they waiting for? husband
and father? son and older brother?

or her most recent boyfriend?
Downstairs at the carrousel, waiting
for my aunt's suitcase, I saw the
boy wearing an army jacket
with three stripes and one rocker.

2　Will someone please explain to me
how rawboned Oklahoma and
North Texas women (dust bowl
faces, someone said) manage to
have all these beautiful blond sons?
The beauty doesn't last, of course.
Beerbelly at twenty–five, bald
by thirty. But for a little
while, maybe two or three years,
they glitter with the glory of
the hummingbird. I wonder if
T. S. Eliot ever looked
at a man. Anything apparent–
ly would have been better than his
first wife. No matter how witty
she was, what you have to under–
stand, she was really quite mad.

3

"I don't want to fling accusations,"
he wrote, "but I think it's time you
realized that for the last eight
years my youth has been a rather
bloody battleground for yours and
father's sex life and troubles." What
he really wanted was some course
of study that would enable
him to light upon some decent
employment. Poets are always
looking for this sort of job. By
decent they mean something that pays
well enough but won't detract from
the business of writing poetry.

Hart Crane's final break with his
mother didn't occur until
eight years later when she tried to
keep him from getting a small
inheritance from his grandmother.
"Nervous strain or simple hysterics
could never explain the under–
handed and insatiable
vanity that has inspired her
attempt to crush her nearest of
kin. And all for a bucketful
of cash!" He asked friends not to let
his mother know his whereabouts.

4   A person who liked tearooms said
he always stood in front of a
urinal while loitering or
having sex, in case someone like
the vice squad came in, so he could
pretend to be taking a leak.
Which neatly explicates "and love
A burnt match skating in a
urinal." What Hart Crane would have
seen and smelled Saturday nights. Down
on his knees, doing the subway
tearooms from one end of Manhattan
to the other. The same poet
who stood on the Brooklyn Bridge and
boasted the entire North Atlantic
fleet had passed between his legs.

After such knowledge, what forgive-
ness? The job of teaching poetry
to college freshmen is vastly
overrated. Helen Vendler
deserves our sympathy for liking
with so much enthusiasm
the later poems of Wallace
Stevens. While the rest of us are
content to be disappointed
looking for more poems like "Sunday
Morning" and not finding them.

5   Mother was in the hospital
       again with her back, humped over
       from osteoporosis. X–rays
       confirmed a new fracture and bed
       rest was prescribed. But my brother,
       who goes to the Christian Science
       reading room everyday and buys
       the *Monitor,* told me mother's
       pain was caused by her medicine,
       all those calcium tablets she
       takes, and the fracture occurred
       after she went to the hospital.

6 Are all Christian Scientists like
this or just the ones I've met? My
grandmother's sister Doll was a
Christian Science practitioner.
Cards and letters gave the address
of a residence hotel in
Hollywood. She stopped in Carthage
once on her way back from Boston
and the Mother Church, and took me
to Sunday service in the local
church. The lesson was against
mesmerism which the Founder
apparently thought was a very
big problem. There were six people
at the Wednesday night service. Aunt
Doll felt obliged to say something.
She told how she had paid her bills
and raised her children with the aid
of Christian Science. And without
a husband. After her divorce
she changed the pronunciation
of her name from KEN-nel to kuh-NELL,
but not the spelling. Aunt Doll
is dead. The small congregation
also died or moved away. The
brick building, back of the public
library, was taken over by
a doctor for his fancy hair

transplant salon. He has since moved
to St. Louis. And the building,
which he owns, is again vacant.

22

7   A color photograph taken
     at the time of Aunt Doll's visit
     shows her and grandmother and their
     brothers Fred and Emmett standing
     in front of grandmother's house.
     A flaw in the negative makes it
     look like a hole is burning in
     Uncle Emmett's pants where his cock
     ought to be. He served two years
     in Kansas for messing around
     with a teenage prostitute, and got
     mercury shots for his syphilis.
     The only male in our family
     convicted of being a man.

8   Kurt is the middle son of a
     Christian Science mother. Eight years
     between each of them, according
     to Kurt, one for each time she let
     his father approach her bed. They
     divorced when Kurt was eleven.
     The oldest escaped into the
     army. The youngest was too young
     to know what was going on. But
     Kurt got it all. How his father
     deliberately mistreated
     his mother and made demands she
     couldn't possibly satisfy.
     No decent woman, she told Kurt,
     ever enjoys that sort of thing.

     But Kurt's father really loved his
     mother and never got over
     the divorce. He drank orange juice
     and vodka. When Kurt was a freshman
     in college, the dean of men woke
     him in the dormitory one
     night and took him to his office
     to tell him his father had
     committed suicide. His money,
     several hundred thousand dollars,
     is in a trust which Kurt's mother
     controls. All of it goes to

the Mother Church after she dies.
A question of spending it now
since there will be nothing later.

Kurt was always moving away
from his mother, then back in with
her. One time it was a Buick
convertible. Another time
the reconditioned twelve foot
piano from the symphony. Kurt
cleaned the copper-wound bass strings
with Twinkle, killing them dead as
a doornail, costing one hundred
dollars each to replace. When Kurt
and his mother came to my place
for dinner, she stopped in front of
an etching by a friend of mine.
It shows a naked woman with
a slave bracelet on her arm.
The man next to her also is
naked. (They look like my friend
and his mother, another story.)
Three figures in the lower right
corner are taking a leak. At
least their hands are down there, holding
on to something. After looking
at the etching awhile, Kurt's
mother said the foliage at the top
of the picture was very nice.

9   If the real things in life are all
     SPIRITUAL, the problem is
     how to handle certain aspects
     of existence. A young man writes
     "The Playboy Advisor" wanting
     to know why sex has to be so
     messy. A woman wants to know
     what to do with the ejaculate.
     The replies seem flippant rather
     than helpful. Perhaps they think the
     correspondents are putting them on.

10   When their older son came home
from the navy, he announced to
friends and family he was gay.
Friends took the news easily enough
but his parents took it pretty
hard. After much soul-searching
and consulting with the pastor
of their church, they decided to
disown him. To kick him out of
the family business. And to rally
round their younger son. What they
didn't know was that this son, still
in high school, had asked his brother
to buy him muscle books. And was
hustling Friday and Saturday nights
on Polk Street in San Francisco.

11   I belong to the older
generation that is queer, not
gay. Though Donald Webster Cory
(a pseudonym) had a chapter
"Take My Word for It" in his book
Homosexual in America.
I sent off to New York for it,
a great relief to find out I
wasn't the only person in
the world that way. Not even as
it turned out the only one in
my home town. After I went away
to college, the *Press* reported
a scandal involving high school
boys, my mother's hairdresser Maurice,
the mayor (married with two grown
daughters), and the sports reporter
for the *Press.* There was a reason,
after all, why he liked being
in the locker room after games
when players were taking showers.
He disappeared but the other
two avoided prosecution by
going to Kansas City
for psychiatric treatment.

I loaned my copy of Cory's book
to a friend, who had it lifted

from him by a Methodist
minister he met sunbathing
at Lake Calhoun. I like to think
the book did some good. Specially
on days when the minister took
an active interest in the men
and boys in his congregation.

12   He had been an exchange student
living with an American
family while going to high school
in Tulsa, Oklahoma. But was
born in Paris, France, and spoke
with a funny French accent to
prove it. He was studying Chinese
in college. Chinese writing,
Chinese history, Chinese culture,
Chinese art. Which is about as
far as you can get from Tulsa,
Oklahoma. Or Paris, France.

Friends at Stanford called him Anal,
Son of Oral. The way children
know how to hurt. Because of his
proclivities, including older
men. Because rumor said he was
actually the son of a famous
TV preacher and faith healer:
"Place your hands on your TV set.
Let His power flow through to you."

The family owned a vacation
house in Newport Beach overlooking
the ocean. Whenever he
wanted to use it he phoned the
housekeeper who came over

to open up and air it out. He
and friends from school would drive down
for the weekend, a beerbust and
other activities. When his
father found out he was seeing
a Freudian psychologist
he cut off his funds, forcing him
to drop out of school. Last heard
he went off to read broadcasts in
Polish for Radio Free Europe.

13   There is a footnote. Several years
ago I read in the newspapers
that one of the preacher's sons, married
and an interior decorator,
sat in his car and put a bullet
in his heart. If this was in fact
the person that I met, I hope the son
is now at peace with his father,
the father reconciled to his son.

14   "Driving back from Marin at night,
we had just come through the tunnel
approaching the bridge. When father
looked over at the lights of San
Francisco and said, 'Ah! Fairyland!'
I wondered if he was trying
to tell me something." His father
is a minister, the owner of
a magazine sold in the backs
of Protestant churches, without
denominational support.
After he finished graduate
studies his father sent him to
Spain, to lie on the beaches and
write his dissertation. This was
the same person who said parents
are taught humility if their
children are still dependent on
them. After the children are thirty.

15 "I had to go all the way to
Springfield for a psychiatric
examination, preliminary
to becoming a pre-theo. At
that time there weren't many doctors
like him in that part of the
country. I asked how he became
interested in psychiatry.
He said you don't become aware
you have a mind till something goes
wrong with it. That's when I changed
my major to psychology."

These were the repressed fifties and
sixties. Before psychiatrists
voted to drop being queer from
their list of diseases. He thought
he had to go straight in order
to be cured. In his case that meant
giving up Bayshore Freeway between
Moffett Field and San Francisco,
Highway 1 between Fort Ord
and Monterey. "This blond sailor
was waiting for a ride outside
Moffett. Three cars ahead of me
stopped before I could get to him."

He is now a professor of rat

psychology at a Midwestern
university. The proud father
of two young daughters. And donates
two nights a week counseling
disturbed adults and children. "Well,
is it a disease or isn't it?
Doctors don't vote for a virus."
His letters indicate he knows
where the local gay action is.
What his wife knows is, of course,
her business. Nobody else's.

16   "All your life while you're growing up
your mother keeps after you to
date men who will respect you, who
will wait till after you're married
to go to bed. And all your life
all you meet are men who can't keep their
hands off you, who all they want
is to fuck. Then you meet this man
who doesn't even offer to
kiss on the first date, who knows all
the exciting things to do and
places to go, like shows and films
and restaurants, but most of all
treats you like a person, who thinks
you have a brain, who actually
enjoys listening to what you have
to say. Suddenly here is a man
you can like and your mother also
approves of. It's hard not to get
engaged. What mothers should tell their
daughters is if he doesn't want
you for your body, he doesn't want
you at all." That was a long
time ago. Her own daughter is
now twenty-one and on her own.
I wonder what she said to her.

17   She grew up in Chicago, across
from the Lincoln Park Zoo. Lions
roared every morning outside her
bedroom window. Now she was
moving back there after living
in San Francisco for ten years.
"The nicest thing about becoming
reacquainted with your parents,"
she said, "is finding out all those
opinions you had about them
as a child were exactly right,
that they weren't teenage rebellion.
My mother is an absolutely
horrible person." In spite of
which she let her mother and step-
father buy them a house and help
break up her marriage. I don't know
if drinking became a problem
before or after the divorce.

18   She waited till her boyfriend was
      sound asleep before emptying
      his gun into his heart. Then called
      her mother who called a lawyer
      who notified the police. She
      went to jail and her two children,
      deprived of their father and at
      least temporarily of their
      mother, went to live with their grand-
      mother. While her daughter waits in
      jail, it's the mother that concerns us.

19   She had a high IQ—her teachers
said so—and got straight A's. At least
through her sophomore year of college
when she began going to black
bars and nightclubs, to Saint James
Apostolic Church of Jesus Christ
Holiness. For the music and
company, she said, and because
it was considered daring in
the early fifties for a white
girl to do. After graduation
she married an unemployed black
machinist and moved downtown. Three
daughters in three years. "He didn't
believe in birth control." And put
her education to work. First
in a hamburger place waiting
tables. Then on the assembly
line in an auto parts factory,
working her way up to union
rep on the grievance committee.

Her husband would buy a fifth of
gin every Friday night. And sit
out front in summer on the steps,
drinking with the neighbors. Then come
inside and beat her up. He drank
other days of the week and beat

her up those days also. She tried,
she said, to understand this was
the result of white prejudice,
years of white economic
subjugation, his need to be
the head of his family. But when
he started beating their daughters,
she took the girls and moved back home.

Starting over she took a test
and got a job, this time working
for the government. "After the
factory, it was like a vacation."
And rented a place on Hayes near
Divisadero so she could
raise her daughters as blacks. So they
would grow up knowing about their
heritage from their father. Even
though they have red hair, white skin
as far as I can tell, and freckles.
Her daughters accuse her of
being prejudiced against blacks.
She, of course, claims to understand
blacks, having married one of them.

20   The daughter did not wait idly
in jail. With help from a fellow
prisoner she was pregnant. And her
mother worried whether she would
come to trial before her condition
became obvious, the district
attorney having decided to
charge her with first degree murder.
She claimed self-defense, the problem
being he was sound asleep. Her
mother hired a famous lawyer
to head the defense team. Someone
specializing coast-to-coast
defending abused and battered
wives and girlfriends. Dead women not
needing lawyers, only funerals.

The judge scheduled the trial for three
weeks but it lasted only two.
Mother and sisters attended
everyday, as did the dead man's
family, his brothers and his
father. Pictures taken at the time
of her arrest showed her body
covered with large welts and dark blue
bruises. Testimony brought out
the fact he threatened to harm
even kill her sisters and mother

if she tried to contact them.
Older black women on the jury
wanted at first to hold out for
first degree murder. They had been
beaten by husbands and boyfriends
and thought the defendant should have
put up with it too. But two men
who were sympathetic convinced
them and the others to vote for
a lesser charge. The judge, after
reading the probation report,
gave her a five year suspended
sentence, he said, so she could stay
home and take care of her children.

22 "Having gotten away with murder
you would think she would have sense
enough to have her baby and
leave well enough alone." I think
she is following a family
tradition, and tried to avoid
the mother as much as possible.
But her daughter was arrested
again. This time walking out of
a store, wearing a fake white fur
coat she was trying on. The district
attorney rushed to have the
suspension revoked. She is now
in prison serving out her sentence
with credit for time already
spent in jail. Her mother has all
three children, and blames everything
on the dead man's family, pressure
brought on the district attorney.
"I raised three children of my own.
Why should I have to raise three more?"

22   Edward R. Murrow, it was, had
a five minute radio program
"This I Believe" where famous
people would state their beliefs in
harmless generalities and
always end on a hopeful note,
just the right amount of uplift
for commuters caught in traffic,
wondering what they were doing
there. Murrow also had a
television program "Person
to Person" where it looked like he
was interviewing famous people
in their homes. He would sit to one
side of the screen, a cigarette
in his hand, and you could look right
into a famous person's home.
Murrow would ask questions and the
famous person would answer them,
even though you knew the program
was rehearsed. Questions and answers
planned weeks or months in advance.

I remember one Christmas Murrow
interviewed Mahalia Jackson
in her Chicago home. Filled for
the occasion with black children
dressed in their Sunday best, the

little girls' hair pulled back so tight
in pigtails, it looked like their scalps
would scream. Mahalia gave each child
a great big cookie nearly as big
as the child's face. They all looked
so cute, you couldn't understand
how some people could object to
having these children in their schools.

I don't remember if Mahalia
Jackson sang any songs on this
program, though her rendition of
"Silent Night" is so beautiful
it brings tears to the eyes. Which is
strange the good news of Christ's birth
should also be sad. Perhaps because
of all the things we know are
going to happen to him, his birth
containing his crucifixion.
But also because of all the things
Christians have done to each other
and everybody else for two
thousand years. Given the means
and opportunity, men have
always behaved ferociously
towards other men. Perhaps this is
the only lesson to be learned
from the Holocaust. As witness
the inability of Israel,
the government and its people,
to think of Arabs as human
beings. Someone speculated

the Second Coming already
occurred. That Christ returned to earth.
But when he saw and heard all the things
preachers were doing and saying
in his name, he got disgusted
and left. I can believe that.

23 I believe life is a dubious
    gift, a heavy burden of
    ignorance and stupidity, passed
    with enmity and vengeance from
    one generation to the next.
    What the Bible means by sins of
    the parents to the third and fourth
    even the last generation.

    "My four year old was watching
    'Sesame Street' when the announcer
    said, 'U P Up.' And he said, 'Oh,
    no, I pee down.' I rolled on the
    floor. I couldn't stop laughing.
    He was completely serious."

24   His mother was seventeen years
         old when she married his father,
         according to George, in order
         to get away from her German
         mother who wouldn't let her dance
         or date or wear lipstick. In the
         middle of the Depression the
         Greek owner of the only cafe
         in a small town outside Tulsa
         must have seemed well off, even rich
         to her. What she apparently
         couldn't stand was having this bald
         middle-aged potbellied man in
         bed with her touching her. When George
         was one month old she killed herself.

         His father gave George to his mother's
         older sister, married with two
         children, to raise as her own. Not
         that his father deserted George
         entirely. He owned a succession
         of bars and restaurants across
         Oklahoma and New Mexico,
         but always sent money for George.
         Which supported the family till
         World War II when his aunt's husband
         could find steady work in the oil
         fields. After George grew up he

got to know his father and his
Greek relatives. But only
long enough to have to make the
decision about pulling the plug
on his father who had a whole
catalog of ailments: high blood
pressure, a bad heart, emphysema,
pneumonia, and kidney failure.

After paying all the doctor
and hospital bills and for the
funeral, George had just enough
money left over for the down
payment on a black MG. Driving
drunk one night on the dirt road back
to the Powerhouse, he drove the car
into a prune orchard, smashing
the front end. Since he couldn't
afford car payments and pay for
the repairs, George let his entire
inheritance from his father
go back to the finance company.

25   Friday afternoon I caught the
     last shuttle bus from Woodlawn to
     the Department. A taxi from
     there to Saint Jennifer's in NE.
     During the Washington riots
     an old woman, George said, one of
     two blacks in the congregation,
     stood in front of the church. Waving
     a revolver at the crowd. Shouting
     "Nobody's going to burn Saint
     Jenny's" or words to that effect.
     Church and three story rectory
     were separated by a small yard,
     both built of that yellow-black
     sandstone you can see all over
     Washington. A good reason for
     painting the White House even if
     the British hadn't burned it.

     George was at work but I was
     taken inside and introduced to
     Father Jeffrey. I hate kissy-poo
     Episcopal priests, their warm soft
     hands. Who use their position as
     an excuse to kiss men and boys
     smack on the lips. The rectory
     was cluttered with odds and ends of
     furniture. Gifts, Father Jeffrey

said, from former parishioners,
including an African gray
parrot on top of the icebox.
And two lion hounds carefully
folding and unfolding their legs
to keep from knocking over lamps
and tables. The biggest game they
chased was squirrels on top of the
church roof, leaping over a German
shepherd puppy in their haste to
get out the kitchen door. When George
got home he showed me in the base-
ment where slave quarters had been.

Talk at dinner was political.
That is, Father Jeffrey and Joe,
a lawyer from New York, gossiped
about the wives of presidents.
Fresh out of law school Joe had worked
on legislation for the New
Deal. And as a young man Father
Jeffrey—there was a picture on
his dresser of him in dark knitted
trunks and white tank top—had been
personal chaplain to Eleanor
Roosevelt. Both men liked Bess
Truman because she kept her name
out of the papers. But if you
needed a fourth for bridge, all you
had to do was call the White House.
Neither would say anything good
about the current first lady.

But this was before Watergate
when she proved she could rise to
the level of the office even
if her husband couldn't. After
dinner George and the Chinese cook,
the owner of the puppy, crossed
hands and arms to make a fireman's
seat. And carried Joe, whose heart was
too weak to climb stairs, up to bed.

26
Sunday morning Father Jeffrey
looked absolutely splendid, dressed
in Ionian white and gold. More
vestments, George said, than the bishop
himself. And at Easter a live
paschal lamb which not even
the pope has. After mass Father
Jeffrey asked me why I didn't
take communion. "I no longer
believe, I hadn't been to
confession, I wasn't in a
state of grace." "You should have taken
it anyway, it would do you good."

27   Father Jeffrey wrote that George
      had been found three or four days after
      a heart attack or stroke, the body
      cremated and the ashes shipped
      to Hawaii. Where friends rowed out
      and scattered them in the water
      at Punaluu. I wrote back
      I thought George hadn't been aging
      very well. At thirty-five he
      had a bald spot and potbelly,
      making it difficult to play
      the role of curly haired Greek boy.
      Not to mention a fifth of scotch
      a day plus wine with dinner. But
      at least Father Jeffrey had his
      religion to comfort him. He
      replied this was true. And would I
      please send him money for returning
      a print, still in its crate, that George
      hadn't lived long enough to pay
      me for. My card that Christmas went
      unanswered. But the following year
      I received a note from his niece.
      Contributions, she wrote, should be
      sent to the Father Jeffrey trust.
      Tell me about the rabbits, George.

28 After everyone left I helped
mother sort out father's clothes and
personal things. Mostly shoe boxes
full of tax returns, receipts for
bills paid over the past twenty
years, some brought back from Tulsa.
"No matter how little we paid
or how long it took, if we bought
something on time we always managed
to pay for it." I went down to
the bedspring factory to see about
his insurance and to get rid
of his toolbox. "The best way would
be to have the boys in the shop
look them over and make an offer.
But don't expect much. They're old
and worn. Louis never paid much
for tools. He was afraid of taking
money away from you boys and
Winifred." Mother hated father
being a machinist, the grease
in his work clothes that dirtied her
washing machine and rinse tubs. When
they could afford it she sent his
work clothes out to a commercial
laundry. His handkerchiefs always
had fine rust spots from grinding steel.

A picture taken a few months
before his death shows him standing
on a wood box next to the new
automated turret lathe. Once
everything was set up, you pressed
a button and the machine did
the rest. Younger men were afraid
of being caught in this machine,
but father enjoyed making it
do what he wanted. The longer
he was a machinist the more
confidence he had in what he
could do. He figured anything
someone else built he could take
apart and put together again.
Men on production liked having
him care for their machines because
he knew what it was like being
on piecework. Whenever a machine
broke down he worked hard to get
it going as soon as he could.

The foreman showed me some brass parts
father made on the turret lathe.
They were mounted on the wall and
looked like bits of pipe. I could tell
they had been machined but that was
all. He said they were really good.

SEVEN
JAPANESE
PORTRAITS

1   When my aunt the Abbess was
eighty-four years old, she went
to look at the new palace
while it was being built. She said,
"The windows in the Rokujo
Palace didn't peak at the top
but were round and didn't have any
frames." She would have been thirteen
when the Rokujo Palace burned.
But how like her to remember
details which even the experts
had overlooked. Needless to say
the windows were corrected
before the palace was completed.

2 Late one night a message came
from the Regent himself. I said
I would go immediately. While
I was trying to make up my
mind what to wear, another
message arrived. "It doesn't make
any difference what you wear this
time of night. Hurry." So I went
to court wearing the rumpled clothes
I wore at home. When I arrived
the Regent brought out a bottle
of wine and two stoneware cups. "It
would have been lonely drinking this
by myself. Look around and see
if you can find something to eat."
I looked in all the cupboards till
I found some crackers and a small
jar with a little sweet bean paste
sticking to the bottom. I told
His Excellency this was all
I could find. "They will do quite
nicely," he said. We were drinking
and talking when it became daylight.

3   Father's house had been furnished
with his best screens and paintings.
Even my room had new curtains
and floormats. "Is my room being
used for his visit?" Which made
everyone laugh. "Isn't she cute
when she acts innocent?" But I
really didn't know what it was all
about. My stepmother helped me
dress, three unlined robes and a gown
with plum trees embroidered against
a bamboo fence, on a pattern
of plum blossoms and tendrils. Then
father came in to talk with me.
"Don't go to sleep before he
arrives. And remember, a lady
is always kind and does what she
is told." But I fell asleep any-
way. Waiting for his arrival.

When I woke I was lying towards
the rear of the room, away from
the door. Someone was lying next
to me. "Don't run away," he said,
grabbing me and holding me
down. All I could think to do
was cry. I didn't know how I
could ever face other people.

I was also aware he thought
I was behaving like a child.
"Even though you hate me, please come
out to see me off. Otherwise
it will be too embarrassing."
I put an unlined robe on over
my gown. In the moonlight he looked
much different to me. I had to
admit he was really quite handsome
in his green and red and purple
clothes. It's amazing, I thought, how
we learn these things without any
instructions. After he left
father wanted to know every–
thing that happened, whether he was
satisfied with the arrangement.
There was nothing to do, father
said, except wait for his letter
and prepare a poem in reply.

4   She wanted, she wrote, a husband
     thirty nights a month. Which even
     a principal wife, of course, could
     not expect. But she was one of the
     three great beauties of her day,
     and beautiful people expect
     to receive more than other people.
     Her husband wrote that her complaints
     kept him away. Jealousy can
     cause terrible things to happen,
     but this was merely an excuse.
     Everyday she and her household
     had to watch his splendid carriage,
     fifty or more outriders, pass
     her house, on their way to visit
     that other woman. When they were
     almost completely estranged—his
     visits to her once a year or
     less—they began writing letters
     to each other again. With lots
     of acrimony. Rehearsing
     old times. Then late one New Year's Eve
     there was a pounding at her door.

     Here her diary breaks off. Inter-
     rupted by a visitor, she
     never saw the point in taking
     it up again. But who was at

her door? Her husband used to pound
on her door late at night like that.
Did they resume their relation-
ship? Unlikely since he continued
chasing after young women till
his death twenty years later.
More likely she began going
on frequent pilgrimages (she
had a taste for that sort of thing)
traipsing from shrine to shrine like
so many women in that period.
Her son, a minor official
whose future she worried so much
about, is remembered today
only because she is known as
"Michitsuna's mother." Having
herself no other name or title.

5   Raining. And invited to her
room, a mosquito net spread
across the doorway. A chest of
drawers in a corner opposite
a closet. "Do you think it will
be OK?" "Why shouldn't it be
OK? I can't count the number of
men going in and out the room
next door." She is, she says, twenty-
three years old but looks perhaps
younger. Since I don't care what age
she is, I'm of two minds. One is
to believe her since she has no
reason for lying. The other
is to wonder why she's lying.

"Let me see what you bought." She
untied the package, expecting
no doubt to find a dirty book
or dirty pictures. Instead, there
were two issues of a journal
published in early Meiji that
I had found in a secondhand
bookstore. "Are you surprised?" I tell
her I'm a writer and she thinks
I must write dirty books because
I have no other apparent
means of support. But I am a

poet and teacher of poetry:
haiku, waka, and linked verse.
What could a young man do who had
a certain taste and no better
alternative? Students come to
the house or I go out to judge
a contest, without being harsh
enough to discourage lessons
or entry fees. "This is not to
detract from the importance of
what you're saying but it's prose."

I watched her make tea. "Is that well
water or tap?" At my age I'm
more afraid of typhoid fever
than catching any venereal
disease. My sister who lives with
me says old men shouldn't be so
interested in women. But it's
not a matter of performance
so much as looking and listening.
Reminded of the hours and days
I spent as a youth drinking tea
and listening to them talk. "The rain
seems to have stopped. I'll be going."
"Do come back. I'll give you my card."

6   A murderer kills human flesh,
    but what do you call a man who
    assassinates the soul? The boy
    was eighteen and attached himself
    to a Christian school, working as
    a janitor in order to learn
    English, when he went to the
    missionary he trusted most
    and told him his plans. "What, you
    intend going to America?"
    The missionary's wife was in
    the room and also sneered at him.
    Next morning he ran away, his
    possessions tied in a cloth square.

    "Even murderers," he wrote years
    afterwards, "I may forgive
    according to their condition.
    But about sneering there is no
    excuse. Because no one can sneer
    at innocent people without
    being intentionally in-
    sincere. That missionary and
    his wife tried to assassinate
    my soul. I had a great pain in
    my heart which cried out, why you?"

    Time did nothing to lessen

the pain, which remained as sharp
as ever when he remembered
what happened. But few Japanese
today would probably want to
react that way. Since then we've had
much more experience dealing
with foreigners. We've learned they can't
be expected to follow the rules
of normal human conduct.

7   It doesn't excuse his rudeness
or the impropriety of his
words. But you must reflect on
the fact he was already resolved
to die if Japan surrendered.
It must have been difficult day
after day dealing with men
who unlike him were willing to
accept the humiliation of
defeat. Without even the dream
of a final battle. "The Prince
will do nothing unless there's a
definite plan with a real chance
of striking a decisive blow.
Knowing what the admirals think,
I went to see the army chief
of staff. The army has no plan
either." Our best hope, he said, was
to ask the Prince to delay any
action till the decision had
been reported to the Grand Shrine
at Ise. But the next day was
hectic, I couldn't get in to
see the Prince, the surrender was
announced. People everywhere stood
at attention while the record was
being played. Unable to under-
stand a word the Emperor spoke

in his remote court dialect.
Only that the war was over.

That evening he invited
staff officers to his official
residence. After they left, some-
time after midnight, he wrote a
note apologizing to the dead
fliers and their families. He
urged young people not to forget
their pride in being Japanese:
"You are the nation's treasure.
Strive for peace throughout the world."
Just before daylight his wife tele-
phoned his aide. The admiral, she said,
had performed seppuku. The cut
across the stomach was cleanly
done. But the attempt to cut the
jugular was not so success-
ful. When his aide arrived the admiral
was conscious but refused all help.
Holding his wife's hand he lingered
till six that evening. His desire
to endure this prolonged suffering
was, I think, atonement not only
for what he had done. But for what
he had been unable to do.

Admiral Onishi thought our
superior planes and ships could win
the war. When that didn't happen
he hoped our superior Japanese

spirit would save us. I wonder
what he would think if he could know
it's cars and TV sets "Made in
Japan" that have conquered the world.

ROLLERDROME
AND
THE MILLIONAIRE

Well, sir, what do you suggest? Shall we stand here and shed tears and call each other names? Or shall we ... go to Constantinople?

Dashiell Hammett, *The Maltese Falcon*

Rollerdrome

Colonel Smyrl wasn't popular
but he wasn't disliked either.
Considering he had a good-
looking French wife from Algiers, tall
and blond hair, a reputation
for being artistic. Which meant
she was seen in the base hobby
shop tracing W. Steig cartoons
on to unglazed tiles, then glazing
them. One time I pulled CQ at
group headquarters and went in Smyrl's
office. The cartoons were on his
desk facing frontwards. Anyone
reporting to him, standing at
attention, couldn't help but see
People are no damn good. Mother
loved me but she died.

          What happened
was a contractor named Morris
Jaffe built a million dollar
Rollerdrome. Brick and stucco, a
foundation strong enough to
support a ten story building,
landscaping extending all the way
to Loop 13. The problem was

nobody wanted to skate. Not
after marching all day. Their chance
to sit in the latrine, read letters
from home. The rink stood empty
skates in their racks, cash registers
silent.

General Grills called Smyrl
into his office. Ordered him
to let trainees take their PT
fifty cents an hour on skates, their
alternative being to police
the parade ground on hands and knees.
"Three hundred dollars a day gets
the job done." "Can you tell me how
I can guarantee skaters without
ordering these recruits to skate?"
"That's why you're drawing a colonel's
pay. To figure out things like that."
Smyrl refused and three days later
was relieved of his command. The
inquiry board met in the
psychological research center.
"He shows extreme vacillation
of purpose. The peculiar
influence of his wife, a foreign-
born woman."

I called a friend who
worked for a newspaper. And asked
him to meet me at the Roller-
drome six a.m. Two flights were

already lined up to skate. The
man Jaffe hired to operate
the rink came over and intro-
duced himself. "A lot of these boys
have never been on skates. They don't
know how much fun skating can be."
To prove his point he put on skates
and promptly fell down, breaking
three ribs and carried away
in an ambulance. The story
was in the afternoon San
Antonio paper where it went out
over the AP wire. And was
picked up next morning in New York
by the "Today Show." The nation
learned basic trainees at Lackland
were being forced to pay for their
physical training. Air Force
Secretary James Douglas transferred
Smyrl and his wife to Morocco,
sent Grills to a NATO post in
Italy, but approved Jaffe's
profit. The electric sign flash-
ing "WALTZ" on and off. The Air Force
roller skating towards Vietnam.

AFM 35 Dash 4

Considering the fact everyone
joined the Air Force voluntarily,
it was amazing how many
wanted out. As soon as possible
for any reason whatsoever.
In basic training we heard about
the airman who rode an imaginary
motorcycle everywhere on base,
revving the motor, going Vroom! Vroom!
When he finally got his discharge,
AFM 35 dash 4, he rode
his motorcycle to the main gate
and carefully dismounted—it
helps the story if the airman
is also bowlegged—put down
the kickstand and walked away. A guard
said, "Hey, aren't you taking your bike
with you?" "Hell, no. I'm leaving it
for the next person who needs it."

This airman is like the airman
who went around picking up pieces
of paper, examining each piece
carefully and shaking his head,
"This isn't it." When he was handed
his discharge he said, "This is it."

Versions of these stories involving
horses and chariots, papyrus
and clay tablets, were probably told
by soldiers in Caesar's army. The
stories would have been old, even then.

Truth

"A punk kid," he said. Standing
in my classroom. Grinning from ear
to ear. Holding out his hand and
waiting to introduce himself.
Too tall and slump shouldered to be
my type. But I was vulnerable.
Living in the barracks. Waiting
for my wife to join me so I
could qualify for enlisted
married men's on-base housing. Not
that anything happened, the word
virgin being made male for all
practical purposes. I
refuse to tell someone in bed
what to do. So we talked a lot
about music and poetry
and Ludwig Wittgenstein. How the
Tractatus communicates like
poetry even before you
understand what it says. When I
introduced him to Elizabeth
the three of us became friends.

Elizabeth and I met our
freshman year in college where we
both were music majors, cello

and piano respectively.
And went steady for the next
four years. When graduation
threatened my student deferment,
Elizabeth proposed that we
elope, taking her cello with
us to the motel, so I could
avoid the draft. I spent my
wedding night listening to Bach's
cello suites played accurately
with enthusiasm. When my draft
board stopped deferring husbands,
only fathers, I joined the Air
Force to avoid Korea. The
peace talks at Panmunjom being
shaky in spite of the truce.

Our apartment at Lackland was
near the firing range. Sergeants and
their wives lived a little further
off, while officer families
lived at the far end of the street.
He helped unload the U-Haul
trailer. A waterfall bedroom
suite from Elizabeth's mother
when she realized Elizabeth
was married and too old for an
annulment. Wood grain printed on
paper to look like inlaid
veneer. Boxes of pots and pans,
dishes and more linen, also
from Elizabeth's mother.

Boxes of my books and music.
I paid three hundred dollars for
a Chickering grand with a stiff
action like a Steinway, which made
it good for practicing. He liked
Mendelssohn's "Songs without Words"
even though I explained they were
more fun to play than listen to.

He bought a grill at Sears so we
could charcoal steaks. The butcher at
the wholesale meat place laid a knife
against a quarter of a cow:
"How thick do you like your steaks?"
Elizabeth made the salad and
I mixed screwdrivers. Afterwards
we went to a drive-in movie
waiting for it to get dark. One
night this was a Mexican film,
the kind where the girl drops a white
flower in the dirt and a man
steps on it. He rolled up the
window on the loudspeaker hard
enough to break the glass. He
apologized but never offered
to pay for the broken window.

The Air Force being the perfect
place to talk, mostly what we did
when he came over to visit
was talk. And no matter what we
started talking about—the Air

Force, teaching math, my request to
transfer to the band—we always
ended up arguing about
philosophy and truth. The problem
of how we know anything
beyond the propositions of
science. He took the view that truth
cannot be expressed but must be
shown, that truth can be recognized
but not understood. That was why
he believed art and music are
closer to the truth than poetry,
even though he sometimes wrote
poetry. I trust language.
Everything that can be thought at
all can be thought clearly. Every-
thing that can be said can be said
clearly. We cannot therefore say
what we cannot think. Therefore no
surprises. But truth we agreed
is serious and worth pursuing.

Before our first weekend pass we
were marched into the grandstand behind
a baseball diamond. A sergeant
read off a list of all the places
that were off limits. The chaplain
said we might have to die for our
country. No, a different occasion
but the same grandstand. Getting
ready for bivouac. Told to put
covers on the mattresses to

protect ourselves from bedbugs. But
the chaplain surprised the trainees.
This wasn't what the recruiter
had promised. They joined the Air Force
to learn a trade, go to radio
school, or become jet mechanics.

Math was taught in basic training
to prepare them for a tech school.
A quick test divided the trainees
into three sections. The A section
reviewed first year algebra. They
loved moving numbers and letters
across the equal sign. But if
I said, "Let X equal …," someone
always asked, "Where did you get the
X?" It's just as well. People who
see equivalences, likenesses,
and identities think they have
a handle on reality
when in fact nothing is ever
like anything else. The B
section worked on fractions while
the C section memorized
addition and subtraction tables.
Multiplication and division
formed the higher math. If a
trainee knew one plus one equals
two, I thought I could teach him the
rest. But I met trainees for whom
one plus one was too difficult
a concept. "If my teachers

couldn't teach me in ten years, what
can you hope to do in three weeks?"
I taught math less than six months
before my transfer to the band
came through. There I played piano
for rehearsals and carried a pair
of cymbals in parades. When-
ever the band had a funeral
to play, I would get the day off.

In July I caught pneumonia
along with all the other
airmen. And was in the hospital
three weeks. One story wood barracks
connected by covered ramps.
The medics marked both cheeks with red
X's so they wouldn't stick me
with penicillin in the same
place every time. Elizabeth
didn't drive but he volunteered
to drive her over every evening
to see me. Sunday they packed
a picnic lunch which we spread out
on my bed. My copy of the
Tractatus was in the bottom
of the basket. "I don't know if
you know what went on while you were
in the hospital. But my wife says
all the sergeants' wives are talking
about it. Your friend's car was parked
in front of your apartment every
night and was usually still

there in the morning. Something like
this could hurt your chances of
going to the national band."

There it was. A duty clearly
to be done. In Texas a husband
can kill his wife's boyfriend and
get away with murder. If I
asked Elizabeth, she would say
they were up late listening to
her play the cello. Or reading
T. S. Eliot together.
It was more convenient for him
to sleep over on the sofa
than go back to his barracks. She
would be right, of course, but who
would believe her? Next morning
I met him in his classroom. "Our
friendship is over. You are not
seriously pursuing the truth."

At Andrews Air Force Base I was
        Issued
A chrome-plated helmet to wear
        In parades.

Virgil at Pittsburg, Kans.

It wasn't that the poetry
was unimportant. But the poet
was who everyone came to see.
So many people they had to pipe
his address over loudspeakers
to the crowd outside the hall where
he was speaking. When he stood tall
and erect, towering over the
lectern, everyone was impressed.
And when he began to intone
those famous lines that everyone
has by heart, you can understand
why he is called The Poet and
why the President asked him to
write the history of our country.

Afterwards I went to the
reception for him in the Student
Center. Sponsored by the Language
and Literature Department.
I was embarrassed all they had
was ginger ale poured over lime
sherbet. Cookies baked by Home
Economics. Standing there, chatting
with students and faculty, he
didn't seem so tall or very

important. Flakes of dandruff on
his oily hair and on the shoulders
of a dark blue suit. Brown shoes with
two-inch heels. He seemed to notice
the female student dipping punch
into paper cups. Later she claimed
he brushed his hands against her buttocks.

I wanted to ask a technical
question to show I had read
all his poems and really cared
about what he was trying to
say. Instead, he complained about
the hotel where he was staying,
food on airplanes, and the delay
in Kansas City locating
his suitcase. Three thousand dollars,
a round-trip airplane ticket, and
one hundred dollars for meals
and lodging. That was on the voucher
signed by the department chairman
and sent to the accounting office.

Ars(e) Poetica

1   If I had written
         Madame Butterfly
         things would have turned out
         much differently.
         She would have married
         Sharpless. He would have
         adopted her child.
         They would all have lived
         happily ever after.

2   He will come from darkness,
         touch crescendos I cannot
         contain. Love will be his
         hands and every movement
         warm. "Don't croon," he said.

3   The reject slip had a hand-
     written note: "Don't you think
     they're too Idiotic?"
     After I threw the slip away
     I realized she had written
     Eliotic. Both inter-
     pretations are valid.

4   What is so rare as a
     day in August. Then if
     ever Bill Tremblay lays
     it on the line: "It's prose."

5   My poems aren't so much
     written as worried into
     existence. Then abandoned.

6   Raymond Carver writes that he'd
    take poison before he'd go
    through that time again, what he
    calls the ferocious years of
    parenting. But it's children
    who have the last word, who will
    tell what it's like having an
    alcoholic writer for a father.

7   "Well, there it is," he said,
    and meant it. Except I wasn't
    sure what he meant. So I
    asked him. "That is a problem,"
    he said, and shuffled off
    into the surrounding dark.

8   And heard a voice within that cried
"Jun Jun" to dirty ears. I wonder
if that's what Krishna meant when
he stood on a mountain peak in
Darien, surveying the battle-
field at Waterloo, and whistling
"Lillibulero" to himself.

Not Michelangelo's David

David and Richard had been lovers
the year before, walking around
campus holding hands. Now they were
roommates, according to Richard,
and David was seeing someone
whose name he was trying to keep
secret, David said, to protect
that person's job. I could tell
whenever David was meeting him
after school. David would fidget
in class and sit down carefully.
But it meant a real dinner in–
stead of boiling spaghetti in
his room. Eating it with butter
kept outside on the window sill.

David certainly looked like a
starving student. A skinny body
inside the worn-out suit he wore
to classes. Shirts with collars
too big for his neck. Grease spotted
ties. Cleanliness was not one
of David's obsessions. Mozart
was. His collection of LP's,
which he considered perfectly
balanced, included only three

composers: twelve inches of Mozart,
three inches of Bach, and one inch
of Beethoven. He objected
to Beethoven's C-sharp minor
quartet because it has seven
movements, which isn't classical.

David's other obsession was
art. The only person I know
who could get off on pictures
of horses, especially Rubens,
all those lovely rear ends. He drew
horses, he said, while masturbating.
But sex outside one's own species
carries classicism about as
far as it can go. After mating
with a swan, what can you do for
an encore? Perhaps because he
he was deficient in that depart-
ment, flat as a board, David
liked nothing better than to bury
his face in the cheeks of a large
Germanic ass. One summer he
took the bus to Texas. All next
winter I had to listen to him
rave about those cowboy asses.
Texas was Bunsville, U.S.A.
But buns are the first to go. Who
said that, I mean the first time?

After graduation, two years
later in San Francisco, I ran

into David's friend in a bar.
He said David had been drafted
and was stationed near Washington,
D.C. "He's put on so much weight,
all that army food, you wouldn't
recognize him. He even has
a suntan. When I first knew
David, he reminded me of boys
I met in Italy after
the war. Now he's lost all his charm."

Banker

There's a lot to be said, he said,
for having lots of money. Growing
old is so much better with money
than without. When I was younger
I wanted to be liked only
for myself. Now that I'm older,
the shape my body is in,
anyone who liked me for myself
would have to be fantastic,
don't you think? George used to say
he took ten years off for every
Cadillac or Lincoln. Now they want
a Mercedes or BMW.
I enjoy 'em. I can afford 'em.

Arthur and Mae

Mother knew for years that I was
gay. One day she said, "Arthur, what
do you do?" "What do you mean, Mae?"
"I want to know what you do." So
I told her. "Does that answer your
question, Mae?" "Yes, Arthur. I just
wanted to know. I was curious, that's all."

Vietnam Story

Too old for Vietnam but I
enlisted anyway. Who duty
called. An obligation to
defend my country. Not only
from yellow peasants in rice paddies.
What was called patriotism
in earlier and more success-
ful periods of our nation's
history. And because I couldn't
find another job.

            No complaints.
No injuries to speak of. One
week we would clear a village. Next
week they would take it back. Weapons
and ammunition hidden under
their casualties in shallow graves.
Poking the graves with bayonets
to find a cache. Reaching down with
bare hands through decaying bodies
to uncover it. The smell being
everywhere the same.

            After a
year in Vietnam I transferred
to Washington, D.C., where we

wore chrome-plated helmets and
stood at attention for the
President. "I'm proud I feel safe
knowing you young men are on guard
out here." In the dark. Beside a
runway at Andrews Air Force Base.
Discharged from the Army, I
applied for a job at the post
office using my veterans
preference. And wrote long letters
late at night. Proposing marriage
to the widow of my sergeant
in Vietnam.

          What I have said
is true enough as far as it
goes. The main exception being
a high school classmate living in
San Francisco. Who I saw when
I returned from Vietnam and
before visiting my family in
Missouri. I had written him
long letters. Also late at night.
In anticipation I stopped
playing with myself for two weeks.
Took a shower and put on a clean
pair of underwear.

          Married
eight years working at the post
office. Memorizing ZIP codes

and sorting mail. A potbelly shows
how much I like Michelob beer.
The oldest child is in high school,
the youngest started first grade.
There are two children of our own
before I had a vasectomy
in spite of being Catholic.
Veterans benefits and my
salary make us better off
than most families in town. We paid
cash for our home. A chain-link fence
around the front yard keeps the children
out of the street. Most of all
I miss the flat stomach I brought
back from Vietnam. Veins standing
out on both sides running down
into the groin. I am not
circumcised. San Francisco wasn't
everything I hoped it might be.

Lullaby

You started talking when you were
six months old, just words of course,
and using complete sentences
at twelve or fourteen months. One time
when you were in your baby carriage
down at grandma's, you saw exhaust
coming out the back of a car
and said "Smoke, smoke." The weather
was cold, so you couldn't have been
more than six or seven months old
at the time. But you were fat,
terribly overweight. I had
to leave you with grandma while I
worked. She would give you a bottle
whenever you cried instead
of picking you up or paying
any attention. I thought you
were never going to walk, so
I bought you one of those strollers
with a removable metal
tray. You could propel yourself in
it all over the house. Once when
people were visiting you went
sailing across the living room
floor saying "Freddie's going to
pee in my pants" just as clear as

could be so they understood every
word. I never let anyone
speak baby talk to you. Jack did
that to Elizabeth and she
couldn't talk straight even by the time
she entered first grade. But you
always waited till the last minute
and wouldn't give yourself enough
time. I had all your dirty things
the same time I was doing laundry
for Dr. Chamberlain and to
pay for Tyler's kindergarten.
When you finally did walk you
were almost three years old. I blame
rickets for that but I didn't
want to give you cod-liver oil
because you were already fat.
You liked to run and scream when you
played with other children. I don't
know why children have to scream
so much. If they're not hurt there's no
reason for it. One time I was
washing clothes when you came running
around the south side of the house
screaming at the top of your lungs.
I caught you with a bucket of
cold water. I can still see the
look on your face. You tried to be
left-handed like your brother. When-
ever you reached for something with
your left hand, I wouldn't give it
to you which pretty well broke you

of the habit. Tyler never
got entirely over being
left-handed. There were some things he
always did with his left hand. But
he was so sickly all the time
and deaf, I couldn't bring myself
to slap him as hard as I should.

Card Reading

in memory of my grandmother

"Give me your hand." Madame
Adelaide looked at the lines in
my palm, then closed my fist and
examined the creases along the
edge and across the wrist.

"Has anyone ever told you
you have sensitive hands? Sensitive
hands always get a man into
trouble, though I don't see any
breaks in your lifeline. Apparently
you've been keeping your hands pretty
much to yourself."

"How did you become a fortune
teller?"

"You shouldn't call me that.
Nobody can tell the future.
I only read what's written in
the cards. The crystal ball gives
the same information but requires
more concentration. It's also
harder on the eyes. I was born

with a caul over my head
so I come by my clairvoyance
naturally. I used to worry
a great deal whether my gift
was from white magic or black.
I decided God wouldn't give
me this gift if He hadn't meant
me to support myself by it.
Many times I've been hungry in
a cold room without any wood
for the stove when a stranger
seeking the truth about himself
has suddenly appeared at my
door and crossed my palm with silver.
Most people think a card reading
is worth two dollars. A crystal
reading is worth five."

      Madame Adelaide shuffled
a worn deck of cards and set them
on the table. "Cut the cards
and make a wish." I cut the deck
into three stacks.

      "Here's your wish," Madame
Adelaide said, turning the stacks
over. She laid the cards out in
nine columns and six rows.

      "You're light colored enough to
be the jack of hearts but you could
also be the jack of diamonds.

It depends on the complexion
of the people around you. Under
the right circumstances even
a Negro can run to hearts."

Madame Adelaide studied the cards.

"This card signifies a journey
out of town, across state lines,
perhaps to a different country.
Here are important papers or
a contract which must be signed in
another city. You may take
this journey in order to sign
these papers. Do you know a dark
haired man?" She pointed to the jack
of spades. "He seems to be a
a foreigner. You will have business
with him sooner than you think.

"This card next to your wish means
your wish is upside down. It will
be delayed and may not turn out
exactly as you planned. Your wish
is opposed by an older man,
also a foreigner." She pointed
to the king of spades. "You should
beware of him but I don't believe
he intends you any harm. He
is worried about someone else.
He may be related to the
other dark haired man.

"Here is a woman who is ill,"
she said, pointing to the queen of
hearts. "She will enter a hospital.
You are not close to her, she is
like a friend of a friend, but when
you learn about it, it will be
the source of a great deal of
worry and concern."

"Do you think I can get out of
my present situation?"

"I only read the cards. I don't
answer specific questions. It
wouldn't be ethical for me
to give personal advice."

"Then your cards aren't much help.
Do you believe in the cards?"

"I read them for myself if that's
what you mean. I could tell you
stories where the cards have come true
right down to the last penny. Most
of my customers are high school
girls wanting to know whether they're
pregnant and if their boyfriends
love them enough to marry them.
During the war business was very
good but young people nowadays
seem to be more careful. Would you
like me to lay out the cards
again for you?"

Madame Adelaide took a
package of cigarettes from her
apron pocket, withdrew one and
lighted it. I laid a five
dollar bill on the table.

Beloved Disciple

for D.M.S.

Was it child abuse when the
seventeen year old boy fell asleep
with his head in the lap of a
thirty-three year old man? "Leaning
on his bosom" and "lying on
his breast" is the way King James
quaintly phrases it. After supper,
all that talk, the boy wasn't one
to pay much attention or stay
awake. In the two or three years
they had known each other, his lap
had become a warm, familiar
place where the boy felt comfortable
and secure. But was he old
enough at the beginning of
the relationship—or even
now—to give his informed consent?
Had the man taken advantage
of his innocence? Their friends
accepted what went on between
them. At least they didn't make comments
about it. Perhaps they chose to
overlook the only stain in
the otherwise blameless life of

a man who had so much good going
for him. Certainly they thought the
boy, just because of this closeness,
was the one to ask the question
that was on everybody's mind.
Eyes full of sleep, without raising
his head, he looked up into
the man's face and said, "Who is it?"

If the word of the Evangelist
can be trusted, their friendship up
to this point was not traumatic,
caused no permanent damage, no
recurring nightmares. It was
events later that night and the
following week, especially
the enforced separation at
the hands of the authorities,
that left their mark. The boy never
forgot his friend. According to
tradition, he spent his old age
on the Greek island of Patmos,
writing his memoirs and waiting
for his friend to return as he
had promised. "If I will that he
tarry till I come, what is that
to thee?" Even so, come quickly.
Scholars question the accuracy
of this tradition but it offers
a simpler explanation than most.

Crime and Punishment

"I'm concerned," she said, "that the law
be administered fairly by
way of providing equal access."
Meaning that if you have enough
money you can get away with
murder. Two men in Detroit are
given a fine and probation
for killing a Chink thinking he
was a Jap. "An honest mistake,"
said the judge in that case, "could
happen to anyone." Down South
a man is given six months for
murder, to be served on weekends
of his own choosing, in order
to interfere as little as
possible with the normal life
of an average murderer. Mean-
while, out in San Francisco, the
scales of justice are weighed down with
Twinkies. The D.A. couldn't bring
himself to mention that the
double murders were political
assassinations. For fear of
upsetting a jury that felt
sorry for the fine Irish lad
and former altar boy. Now a

husband, father, and small business-
man. Who loves his mother, respects
his wife, and adores his children.

> *"Your father's behavior*
> *gave pain to our Savior*

which is why He made you a Down's
syndrome case." Proving God at least
knows how to deal with crime by
punishing innocent third parties.

Ploesti

Every afternoon around two
o'clock, when the pain killers and
muscle relaxants had their
effect, his speech becoming slurred,
suspected of drinking on the
job, you could hear the engines of
the B-24 warming up,
preparing for takeoff and
another run over the oil
refineries at Ploesti. Flak
was heavier here than any
place else in Europe. An attempt
to shut down the German war machine.
After the war investigators
discovered the raids had failed to
slow oil production, much less stop
it. But now the engines are warmed
up, the B-24 has no place
to go but down the runway towards
Romania, a broken leg and
injured back, a woman doctor
working without anesthesia,
and prisoners loaded into
cattle cars for a ride that ends
in Istanbul and San Francisco.

Grievance

I

1   She can't think. She doesn't read. She gave me all her memos and reports to write without a single clue as to what she wanted in them. She would start to argue with a draft even before she read it. She has no ideas but only reacts emotionally.

2   She can't make decisions and stick to them. She changes her mind as often as her emotions change. Our move from the 3rd to the 4th floor was delayed three months because she kept changing the floor plans.

3   She doesn't have enough work to keep her busy. She reassigns all her administrative duties. Which leaves her free to wander among the employees, picking up folders, giving contradictory instructions, and creating problems which her supervisors later have to deal with.

114

4   She lacks any self-control. I spent most of my time in her office listening to her complain about her supervisors, about the employees in the section, about her boss and her former boss, about everything else which crossed her mind. It became a joke among the employees how many times I was called into her office. The frequent interruptions made it impossible to concentrate on my own work.

5   She holds no one accountable for performance but operates only on the principle of loyalty to herself. Though no one can be loyal to a person who routinely breaks the law and has been posted three times for unfair labor practices. Everything she does is based on punishing or rewarding a supervisor, depending on how she feels about him at the moment.

6   She is racist. She dislikes other women messing around with her men. When I refused to harass a female employee because of her "fat, black ass," she removed my documentation of the employee's outstanding performance. The employee then filed an EEO complaint. Most recently she lowered performance evaluations for minority and female employees so she could promote three white males.

7   She can't learn from experience because she makes up
the past to fit present circumstances. This lets her deny
everything she has said or done, including orders to her
supervisors and her racist remarks. Whether she actually
forgets her prior statements and actions or this is a way
of excusing her outrageous behavior is a question for
her psychiatrist to answer. She never learns and she
never changes but is always the same.

II

A person is what a person
does. What this person has done is
make me work for a woman he
knows I can't stand working for. When
she was appointed section chief,
I filed a formal request for
reassignment. He called me in
his office. He said he under–
stood my situation but this
was a crucial period. That he
was counting on me to help her
in her new job with the move to
the 4th floor and filling our extra
vacancies. That after this was
finished, he would move me away from
her. That was more than six months ago.

It isn't as if I haven't
kept him fully informed about
the mental and physical stress
caused by working for her. I can't
collect my thoughts. I'm always tired.
I lose my temper without any
provocation. Depression keeps
me from functioning effectively.
I've had to help move every desk
and chair in the section. When an
employee leaves at night he never

117

knows where he'll be sitting in the
morning. Forcing me to work for
her shows a reckless disregard
for my health and safety, a failure
to follow even the minimum
standards required to protect the
welfare of an employee. I'm
so discouraged I sometimes wish
someone would bring in a gun and
solve this problem permanently.

III

After I filed my grievance I was
ordered out of the office. And
not told under what conditions
I could return to work. Instead,
there was a discussion whether
I was dangerous and should be
barred from the office entirely.
She has spread the rumor that I
threatened to shoot her and then chop
up her body. This is not true
and sounds a bit redundant, don't
you think? The only person I
have ever threatened to kill is
myself, being depressed all the
time and suicidal by nature.
I just happen to believe the
world in general and this office
in particular would be a
better place if most people on
top staff were dead. But I don't plan
to do anything about this, one
way or another. Sincerely,

The Millionaire

I

The government threatens to fire
me because I want to give away
my own money instead of theirs.
The nature of this giveaway
is a fantasy from my childhood.
When I was twelve I used to watch
"The Millionaire" on TV. Each week
he would give a million dollars
to someone, the story being what
happened to the people after they
got the money. What bothered me
is that you never saw the man who
gave away the money. He sent it
by messenger and you never got
any insight into his feelings
and motivations. How did he
select the lucky people? How did it
feel to give away all that money?
Why did he let the messenger have
the fun of delivering the check
instead of taking it himself?
Soon I began to think maybe I
didn't belong to my parents.
Maybe I was the son of the
Millionaire and he was waiting

for the right moment to send for
me to help give away his money.

This Millionaire fantasy
came back to me about two years
ago. My wife had left and was
asking support for her and the two
girls by her previous marriage.
I wanted to counteract the gloom
about my marriage with feelings of
joy in giving money to complete
strangers. Of course it would have to be
on a tiny scale, I only get
a government paycheck, but I
started saving some money. I planned
to pick names from the thousands of
folders that cross my desk each year.
But I needed some criteria to
identify the recipients, even
as the Millionaire probably did.

My first and most important
criteria was hardship, not just
financial hardship but hardship
in life. For example, a person who
lost both parents at an early age
would be put on my list. The second
criteria was age. Old men
and women can always use a few
extra dollars but I identify
most with the excitement of youth.
For me the most exciting age was
twelve, an age when the world was endless

joy. If someone tried to destroy
that joy or cause you pain, you could
simply up and walk away from it.
It was also the age when money
became very important, a key
to treasure, not just a way to pay
the rent or keep the utilities
from being cut off. When I was twelve
and earned two dollars, I could bike
over to McDonald's, then go to
a movie or browse the comic book
store. Two dollars meant an after-
noon's freedom and if someone had
given me ten dollars, I would
have been in heaven for a week.

So I decided to give the money
to kids who would be twelve this
year on their birthday. I wrote down
each kid's hardship rating. If you
got one hundred you've really had
a rotten life and deserve something
nice to happen to you. I also
picked all girls. This seems natural
to me but some people have tried
to make something sinister out
of it or worse. But girls with only
one parent or none have a harder
time than boys coping with their
situation. It was reasonable they
should get a higher hardship rating.

Starting this past January
I sent each girl a handwritten
birthday greeting on a scenic
note card. And enclosed fifty
dollars. The messages varied
a bit but most said something like
"You don't know me but don't worry
about it. I'm only contacting
you because I want to send you
this. You won't hear from me again."
At first I didn't put a return
address on the cards, then just my box
number and ZIP code, hoping some kid
would figure it out and write me, but
no one did. I sent about fifty
cards before the father of one
girl got upset and notified
the postal authorities. They asked
me all kinds of questions, like
was I dealing in pornography
and was I a pervert. They couldn't
find anything but because of
all the publicity, the govern–
ment wants to fire me from my job.

I've thought this whole thing over
and the only negative aspect
I can think of is that some
of the recipients may have
experienced some anxiety,
thinking maybe something more was
involved. But since my gifts went to kids

at an age when fantasies are
important, when many of them dream
that someday a stranger will walk
down the street and hand them a doll
stuffed with money, I think I probably
created some feelings of joy
and happy mystery. For me the joy
in this fantasy was the image
of some hard-luck kid telling her
friends, "Hey, you'll never believe what
I got in the mail today." The fact
I sent my cards and money
anonymously without violating
any laws or anybody's privacy
and without asking for a response
or anything from them should
clear me of all suspicion.

A supervisor asked how someone
like me could stand to work at a desk.
I told him I got outdoors enough
on weekends so I could sit inside
the rest of the week. In spite
of being bored sometimes, I really
like my job better than anything
else I've done. All I want is
to be allowed to go back to my desk
and do the job I was trained to do.

II

I want to thank everyone who
signed my petition. I promised
to report back to you about
the outcome. As some of you have
heard, the government has given
me two weeks notice. I never
expected to be fired, even
if discovered, since I did nothing
wrong. I plan to appeal their
decision. Seems like if you work
in this office, leaning out for
joy and love is not permitted.
Whatever you lean out with is
going to be chopped off. My being
fired is a disappointment. But you
shouldn't think your signatures were
wasted. Maybe they will make
the government think twice about
the effect on morale in case
something like this happens again.

EARLY
POEMS

Barracks 1177

Night between "lights out" and reveille
Is sixty men asleep, and I am standing
At the door. Outside, to right and left,
Are more lights on above such doors on more
Such barracks. Air is cooling softly down.

In a farther block a guard seeks a friend
To talk with in this sleeping time, but pays
The Coke machine instead. A small red light
Across the highway ignites a fire alarm box
In the warehouses' black silhouette.

The Texas summer sky is stars majestic
In their ignorance of me, marching more
Evenly than we. Sunlight on rising dust,
On the drill field the sound of marching feet,
Repeat themselves in distant memory only.

Before I wake the guard who will replace me,
A little while before I fall asleep
Hastily to wake to faces and obscene
Commands, I would remember other times,
Who I was and what was said in other places.

I am collecting the private image
Of a person important to certain people

Whose friend I was and whose returning names
I will remember before I quit my post.
Let us wake the guard who follows us.

130

What Do You Want?

I want to die, said Julius Caesar,
Staring into his heart of darkness,
A plaster sphinx sent by Cleopatra,
Of carnival nights the remainder,
Stars also.

To a Virgin, to Make Much of Entropy

If Norbert Wiener, Hans Reichenbach
And distinguished other men are right,
Or rather true—I do not mean
Future time with its stark fractional
Coefficient by it, but I speak
Of time when dead men have obeyed
The second law of thermodynamics
And helped themselves to dirty beds,
Saying they no longer need
Arms, legs, or lips for anything
They need to say is said or not
Worth saying—therefore, if these men
This time are true, abandon rhyme
And make so many mornings false
We shall want many more mornings
Of such great making. From pillow
And clean sheet our whispered words
Will time not death's approach to us
But our remove from him. And if
Before morning we cannot make
This second law stand still, yet we
Can make him run from bed to bed.

On the Occasion When an Eminent New Critic Was Unable to Have a Student's Work Published in a College Quarterly

From well within deep wellsprings sprung, late
Poets again set down their mighty themes
Of children born, not born, and fate outworn.
All are dumped in candy (cherry-flavored) dreams.

It has been a long time. Wait and see,
Wait and hope, and let poetic schemes abide.
Brooks-Warren-Blackmur-Ransom-Tate has died,
Leaving the outer world to dark extremes.

Fat cows, small bells, tinkle with decorous gait
Across green campuses. The white boy screams
His lecherous father down, whose life is hate,
Remembering the girl who beams and beams.

After harsh words, appropriate fights, and tears,
I threw him out, unmindful of his years.

Opening Chorus of Cricket Players for an Opera Based on The Loved One by Evelyn Waugh

The River Ganges
flows through Hollywood
sixty-five miles an
hour, where on its bank
weeps our English
colony of writers,
exiled poets, and
would-be novelists
who no longer write
anything more than
motion picture scripts
and publicity
releases. Freed from
hunger, want, and pain,
with lots of money
in our pockets, our
guilty consciences
turn Eastward. Our thoughts
fly up to Krishna.
Our souls yearn for Nir-
vana. But our bodies
remain below,
correctly dressed,
collars mounting

firmly to the chin,
our neckties rich and
modest but asserted
by a simple pin.
We are, if you please,
sometimes Vedanta,
now and Zen Buddhist,
but always cricket.

FROM
ROBERT'S
BOOK

1   Kevin, who reads my poems in
front of me and not behind my
back, thinks I've written everything
I need to write, and now I'm free
to write what I want. He has
a point. Poets, each of us, believe
we are climbing Parnassus, more
than halfway up the mountain side,
the top in view, only a few
thin clouds, when what we're writing
is busywork, keeping our hand
in it, trying to impress any
one we can but mostly ourselves
with the importance of our work.

What I want to write are poems
for Kevin, to tell him what he
already knows: love is real
but lovers in their daily swoon,
Flordiligi and Dorabella,
Ferrando and Guglielmo,
are interchangeable, replace-
able parts. Robert and Kevin
may be convenient fictions
but their love, the affection
and friendship between them, is real.

2   The letter was from this person
    I used to see once a year at the
    MLA convention, known to
    graduate students in English
    as the slave auction, where Ph.D.'s
    without tenure are bought and sold.

    Dear Robert, I picked up a most
    interesting young man outside
    Newark. Hitchhiking, he said, from
    New York to Camden. He stayed here
    three days before deciding he
    had to visit San Francisco.
    His father was stationed at Parks
    Air Force Base in the fifties. I
    tried to explain how it was now
    the county jail, overcrowded
    and falling down and nothing like
    when his father was there. I gave him
    your address. After you meet Kevin,
    I'm sure you will want to thank me.

    Since he prefers rough trade, what he
    likes to call REAL MEN—he's been
    beaten and robbed I don't know how
    many times—I'm not sure what I
    expected when and if this person
    ever showed up, a latter day

flower child no doubt, with long hair,
Nazi medals and a dangling
earring, assuming he made it
safely cross-country. Though these types
never lose an address where they can
freeload. My house has always been
a comfort station to my friends,
their friends, and their acquaintances.

Two or three months later I had
forgotten about this letter
when the doorbell rang six o'clock
Sunday morning. There standing at
my door was a perfectly gorgeous
young man, his blond hair neatly combed,
wearing a navy cashmere pull-
over, white oxford shirt, and khaki
pants, and holding a duffel bag.
"You're Robert? I'm Kevin." I asked
him to join me for breakfast. While
we were drinking coffee and eating
English muffins with Dundee
ginger preserves (an indulgence
I continue to indulge in
even though it costs nearly five
dollars a jar) Kevin confessed
he stopped at a service station
before coming to see me, to
wash and shave, trim his hair and change
his clothes. "I wanted to make sure
you would like me." "And what were the
clothes you took off like?" "The same

as these, only dirtier." Kevin
has been here ever since. And no
I've never gotten around to
thanking that person in New Jersey.

3   When I was growing up all the
       assholes in the world were named
       Larry. These were the boys in school
       who smiled a lot and were very
       friendly, who got themselves elected
       class officer or student body
       president. But if you made
       a date to do something, they would
       show up only if nothing better
       in the meantime came along.
       But a person really isn't named
       Larry unless he lacks any
       integrity whatsoever. The
       chairman of my first English
       department couldn't understand
       the material I was writing
       for him, but he would change it
       anyway. When his boss, the dean
       of the college, invariably
       questioned his changes he would say
       I did it. Which ruined my
       reputation with the dean
       and any chance I might have had
       for tenure. I moved around
       a lot in those days. But the worst
       Larry of all was the one who
       threatened to kill me. Except his
       last name was Lawrence, not his first.

Then in the sixties when hippies
were invading San Francisco,
I noticed that assholes often
as not were named Kevin. You met
them everywhere but most often
at supermarket and drugstore
checkouts. They smiled from ear to ear,
called you sir and offered to help
with your groceries and cat litter.
(I was in the Marina Safeway,
bending over to pick up a
fifty pound bag of Jonny Cat,
when this woman looked down at me
and frowned. I said, "It's for a very
large cat.") If you picked up Kevin
in a bar or on Polk Street, you
could be certain something would be
missing in the morning. Or he
would come back later with his friends
when you were at work and rip you
off. If you actually caught him
stealing something he would say,
"It's OK because I'm really straight."

Now wonder of wonders, after
living alone all these years and
almost persuading myself that I
actually preferred it, here I am
living with someone named Kevin
who is sweet and kind and honest
to a fault, who leaves pieces
of paper *IOU 20¢*

in the coin dish on top the kitchen
counter, who wonders why I some-
times call him George, who no doubt thinks
I'm becoming senile. I wonder
what name Mothers of America
today are giving their mistakes.

4   This young man has read all my
     poems, short stories, and essays,
     even the reviews I wrote for
     little magazines which he finds
     in boxes in the basement. He
     points out meanings, sees relation-
     ships and influences I never
     thought of. He says I've written
     the best poems in English in
     this century. I modestly
     demur: "Surely Yeats, Eliot,
     and perhaps Pound?" He will have none
     of this, and regrets being too
     young to have taken my poetry
     classes. My white hair, he says,
     is perfect for the part. I could
     not look more like a poet if
     I tried. He hangs on every pearl
     of wisdom dropping from my mouth.
     And in front of friends at supper
     laughs a bit too loud at my jokes.
     But such perception in one so
     young, who wears a pink and yellow
     knitted shirt, a silver arrow-
     head on a silver chain, is most
     unusual. What a comfort,
     now that my hands and feet are

nearly always cold, to know no
shadow of doubt will be allowed
to come between my poems and me.

147

5 Real English poets have only
one name: Chaucer, Shakespeare, Milton,
Dryden, Pope. Even the Romantic
poets have only one name:
Wordsworth, Coleridge, Byron, Keats,
and Shelley, though he was sometimes
known as Percy Bysshe. As English
poets get more names, the quality
of their poetry declines—Matthew
Arnold, Alfred Lord Tennyson,
Robert Browning—until you have
Dante Gabriel Rossetti
and Algernon Charles Swinburne.
After that it may be argued
there are no English poets.
Yeats is Irish. Eliot was
a transplant. Auden and Gunn
both moved to the United States.

6   In high school I could never
    understand why anyone would want
    to read poetry, much less spend
    a lifetime writing it. Build thee
    more stately mansions, O my soul,
    as the swift seasons roll. So live
    that when thy summons comes to join
    the caravan which moves to that
    mysterious realm, thou go not
    like the quarry slave at night.
    This is the forest primeval,
    the murmuring pines and hemlocks.
    Then if ever come perfect days.

    The men who wrote this stuff had long
    white beards, that's the way they were
    pictured in *Prose and Poetry*,
    and always had three names: William
    Cullen Bryant, Henry Wadsworth
    Longfellow, John Greenleaf Whittier,
    Oliver Wendell Holmes, and James
    Russell Lowell. Except Edgar
    Allan Poe who had a black
    mustache because he didn't live
    long enough to grow a white beard.

    Then I went away to college
    and discovered T. S. Eliot.

The bookstore at Kenyon sold a chart
showing how all the New Critics
were descended, directly or
by marriage, from Pappy Ransom.
Eliot's name was at the top,
to the right and unconnected,
Godparent and Paraclete. But
for High-Church Episcopalians
like myself, Eliot was an
Anglo-Catholic writer of
devotional verse. I remember
Wheeler Gibson standing in my
room and reading from a numbered
and signed copy of *Ash Wednesday*
borrowed from the school library.
A holy and hushed occasion,
we were finally, I thought,
actually in touch with the source.

7 After that first year of college
I went back to my high school to
visit Christine Webster. The town
attached a bit of scandal to
Mrs. Webster. After her divorce
she took back her maiden name
for herself and for her son, a
lawyer who was state senator
for many years, who thought all third
parties are made up of nothing
but queers and Communists, whose son
was the attorney general (two
years, a fine, and probation) in
Missouri's fight against abortion.
After his death newspapers in
the state wrote how it would be hard
to fill the senator's shoes. I
certainly hope so. But people
back then considered it wrong
to deny a boy his father's name.

I took American lit from
Mrs. Webster my junior year,
English lit my senior. She
assigned only one paper each year
and encouraged lots of pictures
cut out of magazines. Neatness
and cleverness counted most.

As a result, I didn't learn
how to write a paper until
college when Philip Timberlake
assigned one every week. He
hovered like a fearful presence
over the lectern at the front
of the class. I remember his wrath
when he asked a student (not me,
thank goodness) why he had written
a paper using long, fancy
words, and the answer came back,
"to make it interesting." Half the
students at Kenyon were from prep
schools. The substance of their papers
may have been indifferent but they
all knew how to paragraph, write
topic sentences, and footnote.

I told Mrs. Webster I liked
T. S. Eliot. "I was afraid
you would," as if she had kept him
secret from me, which was easy
since he wasn't in any textbook
that she used. Of course, she and I
may have been thinking about
different Eliots. She probably
had in mind the author of "The
Waste Land," while I was still under
the influence of the Anglo-
Catholic Eliot. Is T(homas)
S(tearns) Eliot a three name poet?

8   Emma was here for supper last
night, and flying from the moment
he arrived. Making his usual
comments, attacking Kevin when-
ever he left the table to
work in the kitchen. His attempts
to please Emma only made things
worse. Afterwards Emma caught me
in the hi-fi room while I was
changing tapes. "Well, how long are
you going to go on letting him
take advantage of you like this?
Everyone's talking about how
he's using you." Everyone in
this case being Emma herself
and her friends. I felt like slugging
him and probably should have.
I was already feeling guilty
because I hadn't said any-
thing during supper to defend
Kevin. Instead, I said, "Emma,
darling, isn't your glass empty?"

This morning I'm still upset how
people like Emma are willing
to let Kevin wait on them hand
and foot, serve them drinks, cook a meal
and clean up afterwards, then want

to cut him up behind his back.
Not that any one could call Emma
a coward who had occasion once
to tell the Director where he
could stick his black lace panties,
and lived to tell it. Kevin takes
all this better than I can and
even professes to understand
Emma. "After all, he came out
in the forties when gays taught them-
selves to hate each other. Besides,
he's jealous now I'm getting all
your attention instead of him."
I'd be more comfortable if
Kevin sometimes got mad instead
of being so understanding.

9   It's not as if Emma hasn't
         worn out his welcome many times.
         But he is family and you don't
         get rid of family just because
         you can't stand them. Emma, of course,
         wasn't always the mess he now
         is, a heart with nylon valves,
         insides that are mostly plastic
         tubing. He was nineteen and out
         of the navy when he arrived
         in San Francisco, after a purge
         of the personnel office
         in San Diego. I forget now
         how we met, but Emma claims I
         picked him up Sunday afternoon
         in the Black Cat, which would have
         been before Jose, the only bar
         in San Francisco he had heard
         of. When he dialed Operator,
         she gave him the address, then
         added, "Be careful." "How dare she!"
         But in those days San Franciscans
         knew how to look after their own.

10   It didn't take long deciding
we were going to be sisters.
Emma was looking for a father,
and I was always more the mother
hen and chickens type, since sex—
"an internal attrition and an
expulsion of mucus with a sort
of spasm"—was what you did with
strangers, love being saved for friends.
Which meant friendships often had
the problems of a marriage without
its benefits. The ideal arrange-
ment was doorbell trade, men beating
a path to your door, arriving
on foot, by cable car, or in
a taxi, but getting there one
way or another. When Stan Cook
threatened suicide over the wife
of his best friend, I offered him
bus fare to the Golden Gate Bridge
and a dime to walk out on it.

I felt obliged to show Emma
where to go in San Francisco,
what to avoid. I'm old-fashioned
enough to think someone who enters
a gay bar has accepted himself.
But Emma was attacked leaving

the Oak Room by a young man
in the hotel lobby. "Do you know
what he is?" "Of course I know
what I am, I'm a fairy." Not
that Emma needed any help.
He had everything necessary
for success in San Francisco,
tight buns and a large basket.
Soon he was being invited to
parties everywhere, Pacific
Heights and Russian Hill. With long
weekends out of town in Carmel,
Santa Barbara, and Cloverdale.

Emma found the father he was
looking for, or at least a
Father, an Episcopal priest
from Washington, D.C., and moved
back there to live with him. But
Father was as tight with his money
as he was with his scotch. And Emma,
restless for somewhere bigger, moved
to New York with frequent trips to
Europe, always in the company
of much older, very wealthy
men, all of it documented
with postcards from London, Paris,
and Rome, giving the impression
he slept with lots of educated,
interesting men. When it ended,
"Dumped actually, accused of
stealing his money when I was

writing checks to pay his hotel
bills and gambling debts," Emma
returned to San Francisco to open
a shop on Sacramento, to spend
his evenings escorting matrons
from Laurel Heights to their boxes
at the opera and ballet, their
husbands at home, they think, safely
asleep in front of the TV set.

Kevin complains he can't tell if
the stories Emma and I tell
when we're together happened last
month, last year, or thirty years
ago, or if they happened at all.
Does it matter? Emma and I
are survivors, witnesses to
our own youth, who can testify
as long as we're alive these funny
things were said and these outrageous,
sometimes dangerous, and often
sexy deeds got done. If he had
been there, Kevin says he would have
urged us both to use a condom.

11   Kevin takes this condom business
       very seriously. He and friends
       hand out condoms every chance they
       get, not just on Castro and Polk,
       but in the bars and at Land's End,
       on the goat paths up and down
       the cliffs, to men in bushes where,
       he says, they're really needed.

12   Sex was so much simpler in the
      old days. All you had to worry
      about then was clap and syph, crabs
      and maybe scabies. I had this
      awful itching around my waist,
      under my belt. A doctor on
      Post Street had me get calamine
      lotion which didn't help. Emma said,
      "Scabies, darling. And not from
      any toilet seat. Ask him for Kwell."
      So I went back to this doctor,
      "Maybe it isn't hives or an
      allergy, maybe it's a bug."
      The doctor looked up, the thought
      not having occurred. Clean-cut young
      men aren't supposed to have bugs
      on their bodies, the same way nice
      children don't have head lice but do.
      "I don't think so but just in case."
      Thank God for Kwell and penicillin.

      Now there is herpes, the amebic
      diseases, venereal warts,
      and hepatitis B. Even
      before AIDS doctors wrote articles
      describing gay men as walking
      sewers. No one said colons were
      beautiful, only that they were

sexy. For Elizabethans
dying meant having sex. Now sex
means maybe dying when more than
60 percent of gays in San
Francisco are reported to be
HIV positive. Kevin tells
about Alex, a volunteer
with him at Shanti, who claims
he hasn't had sex with another
man in more than two years. Instead,
he buys videotapes and stays
home with his VCR. Growing
angrier and more frustrated
by the minute, hour, day, and month.

13   AIDS has made Kevin into some-
         what of a lawyer. Or at least
         he thinks he is. He brings home forms
         for do-it-yourself wills, living wills,
         and powers of attorney meant
         to protect lovers and roommates
         from family and relatives who
         avoid their gay son or brother
         while alive, but rush in after
         death to pick the estate apart,
         claiming undue influence on
         the deceased, anything to get
         the VCR and silverware,
         and judges who go along with
         this charade. Impatient to use
         his new knowledge, Kevin is
         disappointed when I tell him
         I've already written my will
         and left instructions for a service
         in Grace Cathedral with all
         the trimmings, and enough money
         in the will to pay for it. Kevin
         thinks this is hypocritical
         because I don't believe in God
         and threatens to dump my ashes
         from the Marin ferry between
         Alcatraz and Angel Island.

Don't be too sure what I believe,
and don't be more sure about it
than I am. But this is the way
our family is buried. The thought
of those pretty boys singing
sweetly over my mortal remains
gives me a great deal of comfort
in this world if not the next.
But being an Episcopalian
has almost nothing to do with
believing in God. The main thing
is promising not to blow up
the Queen of England, but she's such
a nice old lady, who would want
to do a thing like that? All that
kneeling and standing while other
Protestants are sitting down
proves you are physically fit,
mentally alert, a member
of the ruling class. George Bush
wanted to be President all
those years just for the sake of being
President. Because he thought
government ought to be in
the hands of people like himself.
Can any one believe he ever
allowed his Episcopal beliefs
to influence his decisions?

What Kevin doesn't ask is
whether I've named him in my will.
I have, but both of us are shy

about the subject. He's anxious
not to appear greedy, and I
don't want to be one of those old
people who dangle the prospect
of an inheritance in order
to control a younger person.
It being easier to talk
about sex or death than money.

14   We were going out to dinner
       with a friend whose car was parked
       in front of a house where a yard
       covered with bushes slopes down to
       a tall retaining wall. A white cat
       with orange and black spots walked out
       of the bushes, looked Kevin in
       the eye, and said meow. All through
       dinner Kevin worried about
       the cat and when we got home, he went
       back to see if she was still there.
       He found her under a car, brought her
       home and gave her some warm milk.
       "Can I keep her?" A good question.

       Always before I had resisted
       having a pet until I learned
       how to live with humans, afraid
       of becoming another dotty
       old queen doting on her pets. But
       Kevin and I had been living
       together nearly two years, so
       that excuse was no longer any
       good. My answer was yes, but there
       would be rules. Who would clean her pan?
       She can go outside. Not in the rain
       she can't. And try to find her owners.

Next day I went to Cala Foods
to get a pan and litter, some
canned cat food and Ping Pong balls.
We took her to the SPCA
hospital for a check up. Her fur
was dull and matted. "I've seen worse
cases of dehydration," the vet
said, and I'm sure he had. The big
surprise was a surgical scar
on her stomach where she had been
operated on. We kept signs
up in the neighborhood for a week
and placed ads in the newspapers.
Kevin was afraid someone would
claim her, there were a few phone calls
but she wasn't their cat, and he was
relieved and happy to keep her.

Kevin named Buttons for her black
nose and spots, but also because
she was cute as a button. We
wondered how old she was, how she
got lost, did she jump from a car,
was she abandoned, and who her
owners might have been. Since Buttons
preferred our female friends, even
the butchest dike, over our male
friends except of course Emma,
we thought she probably had been
a woman's pet. But stray cats, unlike
vengeful ex-lovers, tell no tales.

Buttons liked me well enough, let
me feed her, clean her pan, pet her
and would purr for me. But she made
it clear she preferred Kevin,
watching TV with him and sleeping
at night with her head on his pillow.
In the morning she would wake him
by climbing on top, reaching out
with a paw to touch his face
with her claws. Emma accused
Buttons of being our child
substitute, but parent substitute
would be more accurate. Buttons
liked decorum in her house.
If any one was going to raise
a ruckus, she wanted to do
it herself, under a newspaper
or in a paper sack. When-
ever one of us raised his voice,
she would run to him as if to say
keep a civil tongue in your mouth.
And whoever had raised his voice
would apologize and quiet down.

15   Buttons' last year was not an easy
one, the afflictions of old age,
a weak heart and arthritis. She
became grouchy, hating to be
picked up, the trips to the vet, and pills
pushed down her throat which offended
her dignity. At the end a cat
who loved fish and never refused
a bite from the table stopped eating.
Was she in pain? And the vet
who before had always said no,
uncomfortable perhaps, said, "I think
she's telling you it's time to let
her go." Kevin held her in his lap
while the vet gave the injection.

After we brought her home, Kevin
placed her on a towel on top
a pillow and sat beside her.
I went outside where a light rain
was falling and dug a hole
between the rose bushes, the site
he chose for her grave. So many
tears, I wondered if they would ever
stop, if he would let us bury
her. But towards evening Kevin got
up without a word, wrapped her body
in the towel, placed her in a box

and sealed it with tape, brought it
outside and placed it in the hole.
He marked her grave with three small stones
stacked neatly one on top the other.
Like early Christians who wanted
their dead saints near them, Kevin says
it comforts him knowing she's close by.

16 What is there about cats that makes
writers have such affinity
and love for them? Probably their
independence, their ability
to retain their dignity even
when they're completely dependent
on people. Not unlike the relation-
ship of writers to their publishers.
Certainly it's Céline carrying
his cat across Europe and sharing
his food with it, even going
without food to feed it, or Pound
out feeding stray cats that makes these
repellent, reprehensible
writers redeemably human
in a way nothing else could.

17   Kevin dreamed last night that Buttons
      was running down the walk beside
      the house and disappeared into
      the roses where she is buried. He
      thinks she was saying goodbye to him.
      Or he was saying goodbye to her.

      Cats come into our lives, make and fill
      large spaces in our hearts, and leave
      tears and heartache when they die.
      So much so, you wonder if you
      can stand ever to have another cat
      but you do. They wander in and there
      they are. Soon after Buttons died
      a mother cat brought her litter
      of four kittens over the fence.
      We found homes for them but kept
      the mother and one son who cried
      so loud when he had to leave her,
      his new owners refused to keep
      him. So far, even though they've both
      long since been neutered, she still puts
      up with him. Besides, no law says
      a cat must grow up and act mature.

18   A bureaucrat may be defined
as someone who believes the plural
of memorandum is memoranda.
This identifies 90 percent
of your bureaucrats 90 percent
of the time with 90 percent
accuracy. If he or she
(the disease not being limited
to straight males) also believes
data are plural, accuracy
approaches 100 percent.

Al Sherman was a good example
of a bureaucrat. Reviewing
my memorandums, he would remove
any word he couldn't find in
Webster's Collegiate, on the grounds
that if a word isn't in the
dictionary it doesn't exist.
It never occurred to him
a word has to be in use before
it can get in a dictionary,
abridged or otherwise. Or that
English has patterns for forming
new words. Al would have approved
Miss Esther Pratt whose students
signed a pledge promising since
slang is a language in the making

not to use it till it is made.

Al was Phi Beta Kappa,
UC Berkeley 1949,
which explains a lot. Also,
being Jewish, he was protected
by invincible ignorance.
For expressing the contrary
opinion about Ike the Kike
and other unbaptized folk
(the Boston Common four o'clock
Sunday afternoon, four above
zero, the ground covered with snow,
his storm troopers wearing black
trench coats, the Infant Jesus
of Prague aloft on a pole)
Father Feeney was kicked out of
the Jesuits and the Catholic
Church, both noted bureaucracies.

19   Kevin asks why a man in his
        right mind would go to Boston
        in January. But that's the point,
        or as much point as this story
        can have—remembering Blackmur's
        injunction that an anecdote
        illustrates its subject but can't
        present it. Though I have never
        understood the difference between
        presenting and illustrating.
        Blackmur, I presume, had the difference
        clearly in mind. The point being
        I wasn't in my right mind.

        With my parents' approval
        after bringing their suspicions
        to his attention, Father Gene
        arranged for me to visit
        the Society of Saint John
        the Evangelist, better known
        as the Cowley Fathers, at their
        monastery in Cambridge. When
        I arrived in a taxi from
        the train station, a portable
        typewriter, two suitcases, and a
        trunk, they must have thought I was
        moving in, an idea the Father
        Superior quickly discouraged.

I was supposed to be making
a private retreat, praying God
would make me straight, or at least
keep me innocent. Both my parents
and Father Gene considered it
very significant that I
hadn't done anything yet. "How
do you know you're homosexual
if you haven't tried it?" is
always followed by "how do you
know you're not heterosexual
unless you try it?" Though no one
ever thinks to ask, "how do you
know you're heterosexual
if you haven't tried it?" Even
the Father Superior thought it
a sign of God's grace that I was
still a virgin. I thought it
a sign of mental retardation,
something that would take me two
more years to do something about.

20 I wasn't all that innocent
of course. I had read enough books
to know which direction my cock
was pointing. And after a boy
in junior high showed me how,
I had a very busy left hand.
All boys do, except those who have
busy right hands. It's one of boy-
hoods great discoveries, how it
feels so much better if you use
a little dab of Vaseline
or Crisco. But how to explain
to a mother her son needs
a room of his own in order
to play with himself and enjoy
his dirty pictures in private?
Though at that age the pictures
don't have to be so very dirty.
Macy's ads for Jockey briefs
are more than good enough. I still
remember fondly all the many
physique magazines I bought
where posing straps were painted on.

21   Wheeler Gibson dropped out of
Kenyon to join the navy. Stationed
in Rhode Island, he came up week-
ends and for Brother Anthony's
ordination, the Lord Bishop
of Nassau presiding, with the
combined choirs from the Society's
two mission churches in Boston.
Wheeler liked serving mass for the
fathers, especially one old priest
who said his private prayers out loud
in Latin but mumbled the English
parts under his breath. Afterwards
we rode the train to Park Street Under,
going first to the Paulist chapel
where converts to Rome are received,
then the Boston Common to see
Father Feeney. The big question
for Wheeler was going to Rome
because his big problem was
Anglican orders, the different
formulas used at different times
to ordain priests and consecrate
bishops. Getting into heaven
depended on technicalities.
"If the orders aren't valid, then
everything we do is just pretend.
The bread and wine doesn't become

the body and blood of Christ."
I never saw Wheeler again.
We never wrote. I thought at the time
his real problem might have been
the same as mine. He did look cute
in his uniform. But Wheeler may
sincerely have been seeking God.
I wonder if he ever made
it safely over the mountains.

22   We were in Father Gene's office
after Michael Tahse and I had
helped with a funeral, the red
cassocks and white cottas back in
their cabinets, Michael gone home.
Coming back from the country
cemetery, Father Gene had
driven like the Kansas City
ambulance driver he had been
while reading books on theology
with the Kansas bishop who ordained
him. The same program to bring
older men into the priesthood
that gave us Bishop Pike, a corporate
lawyer wandering in the desert
looking for the ghost of his gay
son, and could not be comforted.

Father Gene was seated at his
desk, leaning back, his polished black
dress shoes propped up on the corner
of the desk. He had learned to
polish shoes while a corpsman
in the Navy and took pride, he
said, in polishing them himself,
keeping them that way. He was in
shirtsleeves and black clerical vest,
his large Adam's apple jutting

out over the high white collar,
and smoking a pipe, trying to
break a three pack–a–day habit.

Whenever he relaxed like this,
Father Gene liked to talk about
his plans for the church. He had
added offices and classrooms
to the parish house. Now he wanted
the vestry to buy houses north
of the church and tear them down
to make a parking lot so cars
wouldn't have to park in the middle
of Howard Street on Sunday.
American churches always
think they have a God-given right
to spread blacktop across the face
of His green earth. To pay for this,
Father Gene had introduced what
he called modern tithing, ten per-
cent after taxes, a question
of educating church members
into giving what he thought they
could afford. His own salary was
too small for his family but would
stay that way if he hired a curate.
"You can't believe how much they pay
priests in Texas." Christians may
want to go to heaven, but
Episcopal priests prefer Dallas.

Talk finally got around to me
and my problem. Father Gene
had appointed himself chaplain
at the county jail where he
arranged for young men to be re-
leased if they would join the Army
or Marine Corps. It was very
discouraging, he said, working
with the homosexuals he met
there because they almost never
wished to change their behavior.
But on that day when all shall stand
before the throne, sheep being
separated from goats, they will wish
they had. Because, here he lowered
his voice, homosexuality
just might be the one unforgive-
able sin against the Holy
Ghost. Because it means denying
the nature God gave man when He
created him in His image.

Father Gene left Grace to become
dean of the cathedral, then was
called back east as a suffragan
bishop. But the other evening
while Kevin was fixing supper
and I was setting the table,
there on the six o'clock news was
Father Gene, out of retirement
and ordaining his daughter
a priest in the Episcopal Church.

Kevin couldn't understand why
I was laughing. After I ex-
plained, he still couldn't understand.

23   Sheep being separated
from goats reminds me
and is supposed to remind
the reader of two old jokes:

How do you separate the men
from the boys in Sausalito?
Answer: With a crowbar.

Lord Bottomley was found
dead in bed with a sheep.
Scotland yard was called
in to investigate and
the inspector asked
his Lordship's valet
if the sheep was male
or female. "Oh, female, sir.
Lord Bottomley was no queer."

Kevin says these jokes aren't
funny. Jokes never are.
They're meant to be heartbreaking.

24 This morning without any
preparation, nothing leading up
to it, Kevin asked if it's true
I'm really a famous poet.
I suspect he's been talking with
Emma again. But the fact is
I've done more than most poets.
I've published four books of poetry
and only paid to have two
of them printed. Randall Jarrell,
that fastidious man, writing
in one of his annual surveys,
said the poems in my first book
were very commonplace, but so
complacent about themselves,
they shock the reader into
an awareness of how commonplace
they are. Another poet, reviewing
my third book, wrote I certainly
had achieved a voice of my own
but wondered in anyone would
want to read my poems twice. As for
himself, he was trying to write
beautiful lines. I always thought
a beautiful line was one
that did its work efficiently
whatever that work might be.

Famous, no. There are no living
poets famous outside the small
world of poetry. An army
of teacher/poets in colleges
has not produced an army
of poetry readers. An un-
published poet today has nearly
the same chance of being read
ten or even five years from now
as the best known published poet.

After more questions it seems
Kevin wants me to write a new
poem to be read at the showing
of the NAMES Project AIDS quilt.
But I haven't written a poem
in years, at least not one I want
to read. So we compromised:
I will join the others reading names
of those who have died of AIDS.

25   In a country that loves cults
and a state that has most of them,
how very California to
want to join a spaceship hiding
behind a comet. Kevin says
their deaths cheapen the suicides
of those terminally ill and
in uncontrollable pain. What
makes us think they weren't in pain
or terminally ill? But any
reason for committing suicide
is as good as any other
as long as it gets the job done.

26   How disappointing that the world
was created on a Sunday
morning in October, in time
perhaps for football on TV,
but our first parents faced their first
winter without clothes and no
central heat. How much more fitting
if the world had been created
on a mild spring day in April,
warm but not hot, a light shower
later in the afternoon. Time
enough to plow their fields and plant
their corn, then sing a harvest home
before the winter storms began.

Creationism presupposes
something a reader browsing through
the Bible does not suspect:
God has a sense of humor. Who
other than a practical joker,
prescient but not prurient,
would have created rocks to look
like fossils of extinct animals,
or put seashells on the tops
of mountains to fool scientists
into believing the earth is
millions, maybe billions of years old?

Know the truth and the truth will make
you free, and Christians have been afraid
of the truth ever since. Afraid
archeologists digging around
in Palestine will find a tomb:

> *Jesus on the door*
> *Bones on the floor.*

Afraid the earth is round, not flat,
and goes around the sun. Afraid
matter is made up of atoms,
Aristotelian substance proving
as insubstantial as Platonic
forms. Afraid men and apes share
a common ancestor. Afraid
scientists will discover in a
test tube what gays have always known:
pearls go best with basic black.

27   I don't think a person can be
a devout Christian, devout Jew,
or devout anything else for
that matter without also being
a self-righteous hypocrite.
Self-righteous because you know you
are trying harder than other
people to be better. And a
hypocrite because actual deeds
always fall short of the ideal.
For the same reason, I don't think
you can be a real Christian
without also being anti-
Semitic, whether it's your genteel
European variety (Gide,
for example, who said there are
no French writers who are Jewish,
only Jews who write in French),
or our home-grown virulent
patriotic American kind.

Eliot's Anglo-Catholicism
can be understood as a
natural development of his
anti-Semitism as much
as any guilt he might have felt
about sex and his first marriage.
What he and Pound could not forgive

was Hitler making anti-
Semitism no longer
intellectually respectable

"a few cases to make the pt clear
      to get the point across
      everything in reason
          and reason in everything
      (Kung Fu to J. Adams)
"wd/ have been sufficient
          to get the point across

I read somewhere that Germany
was ninety percent church-going
at the beginning of the war.
Neither am I surprised to learn
a Polish pope delayed granting
full diplomatic recognition
to Israel. It's not just his
Polish anti-Semitism showing
(though it's that, of course) but he
is upholding two thousand years
of Christian tradition. On the
other hand, the famous Papal
silence about the Holocaust
(silence which may or may not have
happened) was just a bureaucrat
protecting his bureaucracy.
He probably figured any-
thing he said couldn't help the Jews
but would certainly hurt the
Vatican. Though if he didn't

care much for Jews in the first place,
he wouldn't have had much incentive
for speaking out in the second.
The irony being of course
if Christ was anything at all,
he was certainly a devout Jew,
unless he was also a Cynic
philosopher, which would have been
perhaps even more ironic.

28 I asked my father once why he
never told me about the facts
of life, the birds and bees. He said,
"I told your brother but he
never respected me after that."
I know what he meant. I was
always afraid to ask my brother
what he did for fear of finding
out. Even our sister thought he
was weird. "Besides, you could read."
What I read were bound copies
of *Time Magazine* in the high
school library. I specially
liked the departments in the back,
science, medicine, and theater.

When the Delphus Theater showed
a movie about teenage sex,
males one night, females another,
Fathers, bring your sons. Mothers,
bring your daughters. No children
admitted unless accompanied
by an adult. A registered nurse
in attendance at all showings,
father took my brother and me.
All I remember about this
movie is the image of a cord
being passed between the nostrils

of a nose rotted out by
syphilis. Identifying sex
with disease and death is as old
as Christianity itself.

The Army approached sex from three
directions, hoping to outflank
it. First the chaplain urged the men
to remember their wives and girlfriends,
to be faithful to their memory.
Then a doctor tried to scare us
with gonorrhea and syphilis,
ungrateful daughters in a Shake-
spearean play. But if you couldn't
keep it in your pants, the Army
had GI pro kits with rubber
condoms thick as inner tubes. Only
the most sensitive recruit, like
the princess who tried to sleep on
top a tall stack of mattresses,
could feel anything. The company
commander had the last word.
Religion and science were well
and good, he said, but he would court-
martial any man who caught VD.

If I had a son, which fortunate-
ly I don't, fortunate for me,
even more fortunate for him,
I hope I would have enough courage
to tell him his cock will be
the source of all his pleasure, all

his pain. That his most intimate
conversations will not be
with lovers but with his cock:
What do you want to do tonight?
I don't know, what do you want to
do? What do you feel like doing?
Well, what do you feel like doing?
A young man meets someone and thinks
he can't be happy unless he
can be with that person the rest
of his life, not realizing
it's his own nerve endings that are
making him feel good. Men who
realize this become, I suppose
Don Juans, though there's no evidence
they're any happier than other
men. It's been my experience
that when I concentrated on
giving pleasure, my own pleasure
pretty much took care of itself.

29   "What do you do?" "You know very
well what we do." "I know what
young healthy studs who can keep it
up all night do. I want to know
what a broken down old queen does."

What we do, in fact, is cuddle
a lot, the affection there never
was enough time for when I was
cruising bars, picking up tricks.
I always hated it if after
we had done whatever it was
we were going to do—often
all we did was talk, both of us
recognizing we had made a
mistake—the other person jumped
out of bed, pulled his pants on
and ran out the door. Even when
I knew he had to catch a bus
or drive somewhere and be ready
for work at eight the same as me.

So I was pleased to read that Sei
Shonagon, a lady of the world
even if hers was the small world
of Heian-kyo, held the same
opinion I did. In her *Pillow Book*
she listed among "Hateful Things"

the man who jumps out of bed
in the dark, grabs his clothes and hat
and hurries away. The way a man
leaves a bedroom in the morning,
she wrote, determines whether
to love or begin to hate him.

30   There comes a moment in every
boy's life when he realizes
with absolute clarity, a flash
of irrefutable logic,
so clear and so logical he
wonders why he never thought of it
before, when he realizes
his parents should never have met,
or having met should not have
married, or having married should
not have had any children, or
having had one child should not have
had another. "Then where would
you be?" With any luck, nowhere.

Too far apart as children to be
friends, after we grew up and moved
away we learned that each of us
separately and alone had gone
through the same experiences
with our parents. My sister has
gone to Alcoholics Anony-
mous on and off for twenty years
and her daughter has attended
Al-Anon for nearly ten. Our
brother shot himself while in
New Orleans on a business trip.
Our parents insisted it was

an accident. "You know how he
always liked guns." After father
died, while my sister and I were
home helping with the funeral
arrangements, I asked mother why
she never divorced him. "But I
loved him." It would have been nice
if she could have told the children.

31   *My chat pile kitty from Webb City.*
Kevin refuses to believe
this a real song and not one
I've made up. It's true I make up
new lyrics all the time, but I
remember hearing it played on
a country-western station from
Gilroy when Chuck Schultz ("As long as
you take your spurs off. I don't want
you ripping percale sheets.") was their
announcer before he moved to
KSFR and the Wolfgang.

When I was a child the country
around Webb City was piled high
with mountains of chat, what was left
after lead and zinc had been removed.
Chat was the only word we used
for gravel. It covered the school
yard with sharp flint-like pieces of rock
that quickly cut through leather soles
and cut into knees and elbows
when you fell down. Rusted railroad
tracks and two-rut roads ran between
the chat piles, roads known as lovers
lanes in spite of chains and fences.

The mines are long since closed, the chat
piles disappearing into concrete
and blacktop, water in the mines
seeping into the aquifer,
poisoning the water, turning it
orange and brown, green and yellow
where it bubbles to the surface.
A linguist at Cal, himself from
Springfield, said if you know what chat
is you were raised within fifty
miles of Joplin. I wonder if
people back there still say chat,
or if they even know what it is.

32 My grandfather discovered lead
on his farm, what became the South
Carthage Mine, and sold his rights
for forty thousand. The businessmen
who developed it made millions,
an amount that got bigger with
each retelling, making grandfather
look dumb and dumber. He had
plenty to be dumb about, too dumb
or too cheap to vaccinate his hogs
for cholera. My aunt remembered
as a child the smoke and smell
of dead hogs burning day and night.

But forty thousand was a lot
of money and grandfather used it
to build the two-story family
house on south Maple, painted with
pure lead oxide and linseed oil.
A large photograph of the house,
which hung in the living room, had
grandmother standing by the gate
in the picket fence. When mother
moved to a nursing home, my
sister sold the house and every-
thing in it except this picture
and the *History of Cherokee*

County, Iowa which no one
wanted. She left them in the attic.

Even in town grandfather kept
a cow which father had to take
to pasture each morning before
school, and put in the barn each night.
Grandmother churned her own butter
and every Saturday would bake
a week's supply of bread. Any
left over at the end of the week,
including crusts and heels, was made
into bread pudding: milk, sugar,
eggs, nutmeg, raisins, and vanilla.
After the pudding was baked, she
spread it with her own crab apple
jelly and topped it with meringue.

Both died in their sixties, a heart
attack for him after changing
a tire and cranking a Model T
on a hot day in August, Bright's
disease for her. Both are buried
in a family plot full of aunts,
uncles, and their children. The soft
Carthage marble turns black under
the trees, letters eroded by
weather nearly unreadable.

33 The first time my sister admitted
to herself something was wrong
with mother, something besides old
age, was when they were shopping
at Wards in Joplin and ran into
Mary Lizabeth, a friend mother
has known since they were students
together in grade school. They talked
for twenty minutes or more, and
after her friend left, my sister said,
"Don't you think Mary Lizabeth
looked good?" and mother replied,
"Her? I haven't seen her in years."

It was then my sister realized
mother hadn't asked about
Mary Lizabeth's children or
her grandchildren, that mother had
become adept at smiling a lot
and talking about nothing in
particular, hiding the fact
she didn't recognize people
who greeted her, who acted as if
she ought to know them. My sister
also understood this wasn't
anything new, that it had been
going on for awhile, something
she had refused to recognize.

34   How can you tell a person is
losing her mind if you didn't think
she had much mind to start with?
Forgetful? But she always was
forgetting things. I don't know how
many pots boiled dry while she talked
on the phone or went off looking
for something, food burnt black on
the bottom, thin aluminum pans
melted down over gas burners.

Temper tantrums? But she always
had temper tantrums, sudden fits
when she would throw her purse down,
then throw herself on the ground
and roll in the yard, father standing
there looking at her. "What will
the neighbors think?" Once started
her yelling and screaming could go on
for hours, rehearsing all the wrongs
done to her by father's sister
and the Penny boys, her own
sister, her mother and stepfather,
her husband and children. Then
afterwards amid the wreckage
of things said that shouldn't be said,
she said, "I never opened my
mouth, I never said even one word."

I was eight years old the first time
I remember witnessing one
of mother's fits. Frightened because
I had never seen her this way
before, I started crying, "Mama,
what have I done?" No one helped me
figure out that lost in her fit
she couldn't respond. When I was
older I sometimes wished father
would smash her in the mouth, any-
thing to stop the hateful words. All
he said was, "This is the way your
mother is. She can't help herself."

35   After visits to several doctors
      disguised as annual physicals
      my sister had words to describe
      mother's condition: senile
      dementia of the Alzheimer type.
      Armed with these words, my sister
      took charge. She insisted on moving
      in with mother to care for her.
      The fact she and mother never
      got along very well didn't help
      matters. What she found out was
      mother required much more care than
      she had imagined, that mother
      required watching 24 hours
      a day. One night she was wakened
      by noises outside her bedroom.
      Turning on the light she found mother
      crawling on the floor and crying
      because she couldn't remember
      which end of the house the bathroom
      was. Overworked and stressed out,
      my sister started drinking. Now there
      were two people who needed help.

      At wits' end her daughter called
      me and we arranged for mother
      to be placed in a nursing home
      while insisting my sister return

to Alcoholics Anonymous.
I wondered why she hadn't asked
for help. "Nothing you do will make
mother like you any better."
"A daughter is raised knowing
she's never supposed to let her
mother go to a nursing home."

36 In the nursing home she is known
as Robert's Mother because she
starts calling my name as soon as
meal trays are served, calling me
to come inside from wherever
she remembers I am, playing
next door or riding my bicycle
in the street. She wasn't alone.
Up and down the street, first out back,
then in front, mothers were calling
Peggy! Dougie! Supper's ready!
Food's getting cold! Buddy called Doug
his mother's Shining Only Star
till Steve was born and Doug became
second-class in second place.

After the attendant has fed
her—the times my sister tried to feed
her, mother screamed and knocked the spoon
out of her hand—mother stacks
the dishes on her tray, shuffles
and restacks them, over and over,
the way she did at home. After
every meal she said, "Well, I'm glad
that's over," and we would pass our
dishes for her to scrape and stack
before soaking in the sink for
washing. We argued among ourselves

but mother settled the argument
whose turn it was to dry dishes.
When she got a sink with a drainboard,
dishes were stacked to dry but pots
and pans were always dried by hand.

37 When I was a student, teachers
    liked to compare the brain to a
    phonograph record. The more you
    repeated what you were trying
    to memorize—arithmetic
    tables, names and dates, the Gettys-
    burg Address—the deeper and more
    permanent the grooves in your brain
    became. But any one who
    remembers metal disks coated
    with a thin layer of shellac,
    used for radio transcriptions
    and good for only a few playbacks,
    snapping and crackling, the needle
    scraping metal, is aware how
    fleeting recorded memory can be.

    Nowadays we compare the brain
    to a computer, quite wonderful
    of course but a computer none
    the less. On that last morning
    when the trumpet sounds, God will
    have His work cut out for him. Raising
    the dead won't be enough. He'll
    have to reinstall all the software,
    obsolete as well as current,
    and restore data from backups
    in all their different formats before

we can remember who we are
or recognize each other. Those
who died too young to have memories,
infants and fetuses, will no
doubt live in a state of eternal
amnesia, blesséd without sin.

38   The last time I saw her, mother
      no longer recognized me
      or any one else. She sits slumped
      over in a wheelchair all day
      long, tied in to keep from falling
      out, roused only to be fed
      or if someone wanders too close
      to her wheelchair. Then this lively
      woman who always had words for
      everyone and everything, becomes
      frustrated, angry—I can only
      guess—because her thoughts and words
      and memories no longer connect
      or even mismatch, and throws
      her slipper at the intruder.
      Since she is weak and the slipper
      is made of cloth, no one is hurt
      except a family afraid of
      hurting and hurting all the time.

      My sister visits the nursing home
      everyday, demanding mother
      be kept clean and dry, but her
      daughter refuses, too painful
      watching her favorite grandmother
      taken from her. Instead, she tries
      to comfort my sister and urges
      her to join a support group.

But my sister resists, ashamed
for people to know there's a crazy
woman in our family, afraid
Alzheimer's runs in the family.

39

Michael called twice, the first time
to let me know Jerry was in
the hospital for surgery,
kept on pain killers while waiting
for doctors to make up their minds.
"Is that a white worm crawling on
the ceiling? I didn't think so."
Then that Jerry had burned to death
in his hospital bed. No one
knows how cigarettes and a lighter
got inside his oxygen tent.

Let observation with extensive
observation observe mankind,
but Jerry is denied in death
the dignity he denied himself
in life. But if a man has only
a one inch cock when hard (this from
the banker in Cloverdale after
Jerry spent a night with him),
straight or gay, he's going to have
problems. And if he's gay all he
can offer the world are his holes,
which Jerry did to any one
young or old, ugly or worse, who
wanted them. A county social
worker by day, he did social
work at night in a hotel bar

214

on Main Street, or at the truck stop
where I–44 crosses Range Line.

Jerry had been fucked so many
times by so many men, Michael
and I used to fantasize his hole
must be so large and cavernous,
hundreds maybe thousands of men
had fallen in and become lost,
so many men that railroad track
was laid down in order to send
in food supplies and rescue teams.
Jerry was proof that any man
who lets you fuck him in the ass
can't be all bad. His body rests
in a cemetery on Range Line,
a wooded hillside not far from
his favorite truck stop. His spirit,
meanwhile, restless and peregrine,
roams between the 18–wheel rigs.

40 Men who like women are boring,
    specially their cigars. I've always
    felt sorry for women who have
    to put up with these men, sex
    and other favors. Martin, for
    example, was a definite
    do-it-yourself husband kit when
    he and Elizabeth met in
    the Blind Lemon on San Pablo
    where he sometimes played flamenco
    and classical guitar, having
    sold the car and cameras bought
    in service, living in the hotel
    above Fosters at Polk and Sutter,
    existing on red wine and pills.
    Even his friends couldn't understand
    what Elizabeth saw in him.

    Martin did not, of course, start out
    this way. The oldest son of a small
    town banker, he went to college
    to study accounting but quit
    to join the navy and become
    a pilot. Trained for two years on
    jet fighters, he was assigned to a
    carrier where he flew the world's
    largest and heaviest single
    engine prop plane, weighted down

with radio and radar gear. The
engine developed so much torque
the wings wanted to go round with
the propeller, which made landing
on a rolling deck lots of fun,
according to Martin. When the
ship was in port in Spain, he heard
flamenco music for the first
time and knew, he said, he wanted
to play guitar the rest of his
life. Which was ambitious for a
blond from Pipestone, Minnesota.

Soon Martin and Elizabeth
were living together in her
apartment. After getting her
degree she found a job in
the research department of Wells
Fargo, answering questions such
as how many people will buy
cars next year so Wells Fargo can
loan them money. We went to
a party in Berkeley where she
and Martin laughed at the married
couples, their babies in plastic
carriers side by side on top the
coats and jackets. But on the way
back to San Francisco she said
they had been married for two weeks.

Elizabeth was pregnant with
Jennifer, my godchild, now her-

self a beautiful young woman.
(For her 21st birthday I did
what I have done with several young
women, I took her to the Top
of the Mark for her first legal
drink.) Martin found a full-time job,
at first driving a taxi, then
as a bookkeeper and going
to school nights to be a CPA.
Elizabeth meanwhile took up
Julia Child, bought herself a
KitchenAid mixer and a sewing
machine, learned how to bake bread
and to sew, and was pregnant again.
"If the boy had been first, there
would never have been a second."
She also became bored and took
up drinking. When they were getting
a divorce, she said, "I hope this
doesn't shock you. Fortunately
Martin and I have managed
to divorce each other without
divorcing ourselves from the children."

Deciding she wanted to return
to school and research the life
of a famous female economist,
Elizabeth sent the children
to live with Martin who by this
time had a new wife (his guitars
mounted on the wall above the
sofa) and his own accounting

firm in Daly City. Doing
I think pretty much what the banker
in Pipestone wanted him to do:
go to college, get a job, get
married once or twice, and raise a
family. Thus things come full circle
and the Republic is maintained.

Printed April 2002 in Santa Barbara &

Ann Arbor for the Black Sparrow Press by

Mackintosh Typography & Edwards Brothers Inc.

Text set in Bembo by Sasha Newborn.

Design by Barbara Martin.

This first edition is published in paper wrappers

and in a cloth trade edition;

75 copies have been numbered & signed

by the author; & 22 copies lettered A–V

with an original holograph poem

have been handbound in boards by

Earle Gray & are signed by the author.

Photo: Yasuhiro Esaki

FRED SMITH was born (1933) in Carthage, Missouri, and graduated (1958) from the University of Minnesota (magna cum laude, Phi Beta Kappa). He lives in northern California. He was employed by the Federal government for twenty-five years, and for the past ten years worked at a payroll company. His teachers include the poets Allen Tate and Tom Clark. *Rollerdome and the Millionaire* is his first book publication. *Robert's Book* is a work in progress.